BLACK FRONTIERSMAN
THE MEMOIRS OF HENRY O. FLIPPER

Second Lieutenant Henry Ossian Flipper. The photograph taken in the 1870s. (Autry Museum of Western History.)

Second Lieutenant Henry Ossian Flipper. The photo was taken in the 1870s (Autry Museum of Western History).

BLACK FRONTIERSMAN

THE MEMOIRS OF HENRY O. FLIPPER

First Black Graduate of West Point

Compiled and Edited
with Introduction and Notes
by Theodore D. Harris

Texas Christian University Press
Fort Worth

Library of Congress *Cataloging-in-Publication Data*

Flipper, Henry Ossian, 1856-1940.
    Black Frontiersman: the memoirs of Henry 0.
    Flipper, first Black graduate of West Point / com-
    piled and edited with introducrion and notes by
    Theodore D. Harris.
        p.Cm.
    Includes bibliographical references (p.) and index.
    ISBN 0-87565-171-2 ISBN 0-87565-282-4 (pbk.)
    Flipper, Henry Ossian, 1856-1940. 2. Pioneers-
Southwest, New- Biography. 3. Afro-American pioneers-
Southwest, New-Biography. 4. Afro- American soldiers-
Southwest, New-Biography. 5. Afro-Americans- Southwest,
New-Biography. 6. Military cadets-New York (State)-West
Point-Biography. 7. Frontier and pioneer life—Southwest,
New. 8. Southwest, New-Race relations. I. Harris, Theodore
D. II. Title.
F786.F5751997
355'.0092—dc21

                                                                    [B]
                                                              96-40449
                                                                   CIP

Design by Shadetree Studio

In Memory of My Father

FRANK N. HARRIS

Veteran of The
1916 Mexican Punitive Expedition

CONTENTS

CONTENTS

ACKNOWLEDGMENTS

I wish to express my gratitude to the late Mrs. S.L. Flipper and the late Dr. Thomas Jefferson Flanagan, both of Atlanta, Georgia, for providing me with primary source material essential in the composition of this book.

My thanks also to the late Carl Hertzog of El Paso, Texas, who published my edition of Henry Flipper's frontier memoirs titled, *Negro Frontiersman*, in 1963.

Three contemporary scholars who generously provided me with valuable information from their own research are Dr. Bruce J. Dinges, editor of *The Journal of Arizona History*, Dr. John P. Langellier, director/curator of the CEC/Seabee Museum, and Colonel James W. Ward, USA (Ret.), of El Paso, Texas.

My thanks for assistance given to me by Alan Aimone, chief of special collections at the United States Military Academy Library, and the staffs of the following institutions: Arizona Historical Society; Atlanta University Library; Autry Museum of Western Heritage; Fisk University Library; Henry E. Huntington Library; and the United States National Archives.

Finally, I am grateful to my editor at Texas Christian University Press, A. Tracy Row, whose professional skill is exceeded only by his infinite patience.

INTRODUCTION

The eminent Texas folklorist and historian, J. Frank Dobie, was a shrewd judge of men. Dobie sized up Henry Ossian Flipper (1856-1940) as truly "a remarkable character" on an American and a Mexican frontier distinguished by the exploits of many extraordinary men and women.[1] Remarkable is a fitting term for a man who spent a lifetime surmounting racial barriers and pioneering in numerous endeavors traditionally closed to black Americans in the era from 1870 to 1930.

When Henry O. Flipper won his commission as a cavalry second lieutenant on June 14, 1877, he became the first black graduate of the United States Military Academy at West Point.[2] From West Point the young cavalryman embarked on a military and civilian odyssey of frontier adventure that lasted forty-two years.

In 1916, as a civilian in El Paso, Texas, the sixty-year-old Flipper wrote an unpublished account of his experiences in the American Southwest and northern Mexico from 1878 to 1916. These Western memoirs comprise the first chapter of this book. They are the saga of a stirring life pursued by this unique African American frontiersman.

The last several years have seen an acceleration of research and writing on western history, the frontier military, and the roles of ethnic groups throughout the West. Despite this increase in scholarship and publication, however, Henry Flipper's memoirs remain the only authenticated personal narrative of military and civilian life on the frontier written by a black American to be discovered thus far. Throughout his lifetime Flipper remained a keen observer of his envi-

Flipper in dress uniform as pictured in his book The Colored Cadet at West Point *(Autry Museum of Western History).*

ronment. This passion for accurate and descriptive detail is clearly evident in his western memoirs, whether the setting be the American Southwest or the mining regions of Mexico. His descriptions of frontier conditions, his relations with frontier people, and his reactions to them are doubly enhanced for the modern reader because they were filtered through the mind and emotions of a gifted and insightful man.

Flipper was destined to live another twenty-four years after writing this 1916 narrative. It is unfortunate that he never wrote a comprehensive autobiography during those later years of his life. The latter chapters of this book contain letters, reports and other documents written by Henry Flipper that shed additional light on the life of this "remarkable character." Chapter 3 republishes a significant pioneering but long-forgotten historical study of sixteenth-century Spanish exploration written by Flipper in 1896.

It was Flipper's misfortune that during a long and productive life he was always ahead of his times. He accomplished the unusual, sometimes unique, before mainstream American society was ready to accept and respect blacks on a basis of freedom and social equality. His impressive roll call of accomplishments was to set precedents for other black Americans to follow in future decades. Flipper's battles were fraught with perilous adventures. Their remote arenas encompassed the rigors of West Point, the cruelties of the Indian Wars, and the dangers and hardships of civil and mining engineering (often in hostile Indian country) on the wildest reaches of the Southwest and of northern Mexico. From beginning to end, he waged his struggles alone with loneliness a constant adversary.

Henry Ossian Flipper was born of slave parents on March 21, 1856, in Thomasville, Georgia, and grew to young manhood in Atlanta. Henry and his younger brother, Joseph Simeon Flipper, developed their ambitious individualism and intellectual enthusiasm under the influence of their parents. Flipper's father rose to become a successful craftsman and small business owner in Atlanta after the Civil War, and his mother possessed a strong determination that her sons pursue formal education.[3] During the early years of Reconstruction, the two Flipper brothers excelled academically at

New England-sponsored American Missionary Society schools for black youths in Atlanta.[4] Joseph S. Flipper went on to become president of two black colleges, a director of a black-owned bank, and a bishop of the influential African Methodist Episcopal Church.[5] In 1873, a white Republican congressman in Reconstruction Georgia, J.C. Freeman, recognized Henry Flipper's academic talent and personal ambition and appointed him as a cadet to West Point.[6]

Flipper proved his mettle by graduating in 1877, the first of his race to do so. Beyond this notable achievement was the youthful Flipper's personal victory over the deadening isolation of four years of social ostracism imposed upon him by a "gentleman's agreement" among the academy's corps of cadets.

In 1878, only one year after graduation, the gifted young cavalryman published an account of his early life and West Point career entitled *The Colored Cadet at West Point*. Flipper's book is one of the earliest authentic black autobiographies in American literary history. It remains our most informative and detailed chronicle of cadet education, customs, social life, and race relations at West Point during the 1870s.

As the Regular Army's first and only black commissioned officer, Henry Flipper was posted to the Tenth Cavalry, a regiment of black enlisted men with, except for Flipper, white officers. The Tenth Cavalry compiled an excellent combat record on the Southwest frontier. Out of respect for their fighting qualities, the Plains Indians dubbed the black troopers the "Buffalo Soldiers."[7] John J. Pershing earned his famous nickname, "Black Jack," because of early service with the Tenth. From 1878 to 1882, Lieutenant Flipper saw continual active service in the Indian Territory (now Oklahoma), Texas, and along the Mexican border. He was stationed at such historic frontier posts as Forts Sill, Elliott, Concho, Davis, and Quitman. The young trooper served with distinction through the grueling campaign against the ravaging Apache chieftain Victorio. In every field assignment he proved himself stalwart and competent.

Flipper's salient Army accomplishments were in engineering projects that revealed a talent presaging his subsequent civilian career as an expert surveyor, mapmaker, and civil and mining engineer, the first of his race to practice those professions in the United States. The frontier Army made major contributions to internal improvements in the American West. Often, the West Point graduates stationed throughout the West were the only professionally trained civil engineers in their respective localities. While still in his early twenties and a relatively inexperienced second lieutenant, Henry Flipper surveyed the route and supervised the building of a road from Fort Sill, Oklahoma, to Gainesville, Texas. He then successfully constructed a telegraph line from Fort Elliott, Texas, to Fort Supply, Oklahoma. His most memorable engineering feat was the 1878 design and construction of a drainage channel system at Fort Sill, which eliminated a malaria scourge at that post and remained in use for nearly a century. Flipper took justifiable pride in the fact that one of the officers who had previously failed to accomplish this task was an engineering graduate of Germany's Heidelberg University. "Flipper's Ditch"—as it came to be called—was designated a National Historic Landmark in 1977.

Henry Flipper's eventful five-year military career ended abruptly in 1882 by a court-martial conviction, resulting in his dismissal from the Army. In 1881 he was stationed at Fort Davis, Texas, and assigned the duties of post quartermaster and commissary officer. The latter position required accountability of large sums of government funds within a complex system of Army finance. It was a responsibility for which he had no previous military or civilian experience. Although knowledgeable in engineering mathematics, he had never managed money beyond his own very modest personal finances.

Furthermore, there is evidence that Flipper suffered from the stress of the burden he was forced to bear as the lone symbol of a national military experiment. He was always the object of public curiosity wherever he might be stationed. Moreover, damaging gossip had spread at Forts Concho and Davis over his friendship with Miss Mollie Dwyer, a young white lady who was the sister-in-law of Flipper's troop commander, Captain Nicholas Nolan. The couple often went horseback riding together at both posts. Nothing has been discovered about the relationship that suggests anything other than a purely platonic friendship. Nevertheless, such public interracial social contact in that era at socially close-knit Texas Army posts was a major indiscretion certain to cause Flipper the disapproval of most of his fellow officers and their wives. Flipper's position became even more awkward when a white lieutenant began a determined courtship of Miss Dwyer while she and Flipper were still enjoying occasional but visible horseback sojourns. In later years Flipper alleged that about this time he began to detect signs of plots by certain officers to force him out of the Army, including reception of a specific warning that such a conspiracy was underway. Whether his charges were valid or the product of accumulated pressures, tension, anxieties, and his pervasive sense of loneliness, is unclear.

In the summer of 1881, a shortage of almost $3,800 was discovered in Flipper's commissary accounts. He was arrested by the Fort Davis commanding officer, Colonel William Rufus Shafter, who ordered him confined to the guard house.[8] This improperly severe treatment was reversed by order of higher authority. Flipper was able to replace the full amount of the shortage with funds raised by civilian supporters in the nearby community. Nevertheless, Colonel Shafter preferred charges against him and on September 17, 1881, Flipper faced a court-martial tribunal at Fort Davis charged with the embezzlement of federal funds and conduct unbecoming an officer and a gentleman.

In a lengthy trial, no evidence was presented that supported the allegations of theft on Flipper's part, although he was shown to have been negligent in the handling of government funds. He had made false statements regarding his official account during the investigation, however, and had written a fraudulent personal check for $1,440.43 in an effort to make up the shortage. Flipper had vainly hoped to raise the replacement money in time for the check to be honored. The court acquitted Flipper of embezzlement but convicted him of conduct unbecoming an officer and a gentleman. He was sentenced to dismissal from the service. Second Lieutenant Henry O. Flipper was officially dismissed from the United States Army on June

30, 1882. Throughout the remaining fifty-eight years of his life he always maintained that he was innocent of all charges brought against him.

At twenty-six, a former symbol of racial achievement and now an example of personal disgrace, Henry Flipper chose to pursue his precarious future in the socially indulgent and ethnically diverse southwestern borderlands instead of returning eastward to a society of rigid racial segregation. In 1882, he set out alone for the lively community of El Paso, Texas, on the Rio Grande. Despite his handicaps, he still possessed some positive strengths to face the challenges of his new life. He was hardened to survival in the outdoors, armed with potentially marketable skills, and blessed with exceptional mastery of spoken and written Spanish.

Through determined perseverance, physical endurance, high intelligence, and intensively meticulous performance of duty, he was successful in forging a career in mining and civil engineering. He was able to alternate his professional activities between an independent practice, employment by several large American mining companies, and service as a civilian specialist in numerous capacities for the United States Government. The latter employment, despite his previous court-martial, is testimony to the reputation for trustworthiness as well as competence that he was able to build in the West after 1882.

By sheer intellectual interest and ability, Flipper also excelled in two non-technological fields of endeavor. He became a recognized legal authority on Spanish and Mexican land and mining law. To this he added a scholarly competence and originality in research and writing in the history of the Spanish Southwest.

By 1891, Flipper had established a private practice in mineral, mine, and land surveying. He operated from a headquarters in the border community of Nogales, Arizona. He gained the respect and gratitude of the town's leading citizens when his expert knowledge of Spanish land-grant law helped prove the legality of the Nogales city charter. Thus, few local eyebrows were raised when James J. Chatham, owner of the Nogales *Sunday Herald*, left town on political

*Flamboyant mining tycoon William Cornell Greene, who employed Flipper
as an engineer in northern Mexico (Arizona Historical Society, Tucson).*

business and named Henry Flipper the paper's editor for four months in the spring of 1895. The American people were unaware of it, but Henry O. Flipper had become the first black editor of a white-owned newspaper in Arizona and, perhaps, in America.

Flipper's work in the Nogales case led to his appointment as Special Agent of the United States Department of Justice in 1891. He served in that capacity for ten years until 1901. Flipper performed federal field investigations on disputed land and mining claims throughout West Texas, New Mexico, and Arizona. He was the principal assistant to United States attorneys in the preparation of numerous large federal land claims cases. His duties also entailed the translation and publication of several major works on Spanish and Mexican land and mineral laws which earned him respect as a translator and as an expert in those subjects.

These assignments led his always active intellectual curiosity to intensive study of southwestern and Spanish American history and folklore—topics just beginning to attract the interest of white American historians and anthropologists. Flipper became a pioneer scholar in this field and published articles in Old Santa Fe, forerunner of the New Mexico Historical Review. In 1896 he published a monograph in Nogales, Arizona, entitled Did a Negro Discover Arizona and New Mexico? It was a study of the role played by Estevanico in the Marcos de Niza expedition. Based on primary research, it presented the first English translation of Pedro de Castañeda's account of the expedition and made an original scholarly contribution to both Spanish-American colonial and African American history.

During his frequent expeditions south of the border, Flipper became interested in the famous legend of the lost Spanish silver mine of Tayopa in northern Mexico. Adventurers from all over the world had sought the location of this fabled source of wealth. Flipper made his own explorations and became an authority on the tale. J. Frank Dobie, historian of the legend, believed that Flipper had probably come closer to locating the site than any previous seeker. In later years Flipper felt that with more time in Mexico, he might well have discovered the Tayopa mine.

It was through his reputation as a Tayopa expert that Flipper came to the attention of Colonel William Cornell "Bill" Greene. In 1901, Greene employed Flipper as an engineer for his mining company in northern Mexico. Bill Greene was one of the American Southwest's most spectacular and colorful pioneer promoters and speculators. He was often called "the Cecil Rhodes of Arizona," and "the Cananea Copper King."[9] It was natural that a romantic tale of hidden wealth like Tayopa would captivate a flamboyant spirit like Greene. In partnership with another sensational western buccaneering tycoon, William Randolph Hearst, Greene sent Flipper all the way to Spain to search Spanish historical archives for clues to the mine's location. Flipper reported that his efforts yielded only minimal results: "The only definite thing that all my researches in Spain netted was a traveling direction."[10]

Colonel Greene was highly impressed with Flipper's technological and intellectual abilities and his frontier-bred resourcefulness. He promoted him to positions of great trust as the field manager at mines in his vast mineral enterprises in Mexico. Once again, Henry Flipper was breaking new professional ground for an African American in the first decade of the twentieth century. It was while employed as a mining manager by Greene that Flipper renewed his acquaintanceship with A.B. Fall, whose sponsorship and patronage were to be major factors in the now middle-aged black man's strenuous life from 1908 to 1923.

Albert Bacon Fall was, in his own fashion, as fabulous a frontier Croesus as Bill Greene. He met Flipper during the latter's service with the Court of Private Land Claims between 1893 and 1901 and recognized his multiple talents.[11] Fall accumulated large holdings in mineral, cattle, and petroleum-rich land in the Southwest and in Mexico. He became a powerful Republican senator from the newly admitted state of New Mexico and later the Secretary of the Interior in the Harding administration. His colorful career collapsed in disgrace in the mid-1920s. Convicted of complicity in the sensational Teapot Dome scandal, he was sentenced to a federal penitentiary.[12]

By 1904, Fall had become Bill Greene's attorney, a partner in several of his corporate endeavors, and served as general manager of

Greene's extensive mining operations in Chihuahua, Mexico.[13] He continued to be impressed by Henry Flipper's professional abilities and decided to make use of them in his own enterprises. In 1908, he engaged Flipper as a legal and mining consultant for the Sierra Mining Company, a corporation controlled by Fall. Albert Fall later declared that during those years of Mexican ventures: "Mr. Flipper was my right hand man and advisor."[14] In 1912, with Americans fleeing the violence of the Mexican Revolution, Fall stationed Flipper in El Paso, Texas.

Under tutelage of the wily and ambitious Fall, Flipper's adventurous life was now to be spiced by the element of international intrigue. In El Paso his legal and mining consultative duties were expanded to include assignment as personal intelligence agent for his employer, who was now a nationally influential political figure. In 1913, Albert Fall was in Washington, D.C., serving as a Republican senator. He was one of the two original senators from New Mexico, which had been admitted to the Union only the year before. He still retained sizeable financial interests in Mexico, which were severely threatened by the turmoil of the Mexican Revolution. He relied on Flipper to gather and analyze information on the political and military situation in Mexico that he could utilize to help shape American foreign policy and, in addition, to protect his own investments. By 1913, Flipper was dispatching detailed reports on insurgent Mexico to the senator in Washington, D.C.[15] Many of these reports proved useful to the Senate committee headed by Fall that was investigating the impact of the Mexican Revolution on American economic interests.

During his years in El Paso—1912 to 1919—Flipper did not confine his activities entirely to his intelligence duties for Fall. He also took an active interest in regional history and contributed articles and letters on historical topics to El Paso newspapers. He also did independent Spanish translations for prominent Anglo members of the legal and business community.

The El Paso years saw the birth of a romantic legend claiming that Henry Flipper served with the forces of the highly publicized Mexican insurgent leader General Francisco "Pancho" Villa and was, in fact, "the brains behind Villa." The melodramatic tale spread across the nation. Despite Flipper's public denials and his denunciations of Villa and his movement, the fable was to outlive both men.

The role of Senator Fall's committee on Mexican affairs continued to grow in strategic importance as American foreign policy became more complex during the Woodrow Wilson administration. In 1919 Fall summoned Flipper, a consummate master of the Spanish language, to Washington, D.C., appointing him advisor, translator, and interpreter on the staff of his Senate committee. Flipper's competence and devotion to duty continued to impress the shrewd southwestern politician, himself but a few years removed from the same frontier environment as his black subordinate. The artful Senator became a Republican celebrity and, in 1921, President Warren G. Harding appointed Albert Fall to his cabinet as Secretary of the Interior. Henry Flipper received his reward when his mentor from Mexican mining days designated the court-martialled black man as Assistant to the Secretary of the Interior. This was an unusually high federal appointment for an African American in those days, and A.B. Fall won praise from some black leaders for his action. Flipper served in this capacity until March, 1923.

After leaving government service, Flipper again faced an uncharted future. He was sixty-seven but still undaunted by new challenges. This time he turned to even farther frontiers and spent the rest of the decade in more racially tolerant South America. Flipper progressed from America's first black civil and mining engineer to America's first black petroleum engineer and was employed later in 1923 by William F. Buckley, Sr., at the Pantepec Petroleum Company in Venezuela. His unique combination of linguistic and technical productivity continued. While a legal consultant and engineer with the company, he translated and edited an edition of the national mineral laws of Venezuela in 1925. The economic collapse of 1929, however, cost Flipper his employment and wiped out his personal savings. Age, an arduous life, and this last misfortune finally weakened the spirit of the black pioneer. He sought refuge now, not on another frontier, but near the roots he had left fifty-eight years before.

In 1931, seventy-five-year-old Henry Flipper arrived penniless at his clergyman brother's home in Atlanta to take up residence for the remainder of his life. Here he was greeted by another embarrassing myth derived from popular misconceptions of his extraordinary past. His relationship with Albert B. Fall had given birth to a tale in the Atlanta black community that Flipper had been "the brains behind Teapot Dome." Unlike the earlier Pancho Villa allegations, he chose to ignore this latest fantasy.

Age had not slowed Flipper's intellectual vitality. He kept abreast of the main currents of American political and racial developments during the traumatic decade of the 1930s. He expressed his views on these topics in a series of letters to Dr. Thomas Jefferson Flanagan, an editor of the *Atlanta Daily World*, one of America's most influential African American newspapers. His ideas sometimes influenced the editorials of the paper. His letters were rich in their recollections of distant experiences at West Point, in the frontier Army, and as a civilian on the southwestern frontier. They also revealed the elderly Flipper as a conservative with a strict constructionist interpretation of the Constitution and a firm belief in the doctrine of states' rights.

Flipper's last years were solitary ones. Throughout his long life he was, in western jargon, a loner, and a sense of aloneness pervades much of his writing. There are only two confirmed instances of relationships with women. In 1960 in Atlanta, this editor interviewed Mrs. S.L. Flipper, Henry Flipper's sister-in-law. A former teacher, she was the widow of Bishop Joseph S. Flipper, Henry's prominent brother. Henry had resided at her home during the last nine years of his life. She related that the one-time cavalryman had given an engagement ring to a black lady of Augusta, Georgia, in late 1877, as the young lieutenant was departing Atlanta to join his regiment in the West. After several years of waiting vainly for further romantic progress, the Reverend Flipper advised the lady to dissolve the engagement "because Henry is just not the marrying kind." She returned the ring.

In his thirty-fifth year, on September 10, 1891, Flipper did venture into a common-law arrangement with a woman of Mexican descent in Nogales, Arizona Territory. The relationship ended in less than seven months, after which Flipper declared that he could never bring himself to marry any woman of any race on the southwestern frontier.[16]

Until early 1937, as his eighty-first birthday approached, Flipper had enjoyed exceptionally good health. In a letter of March 10, 1939, to a business associate from the Venezuela years, however, Flipper reported that:

I have been sick since February 2, 1937, although in all that time I have not spent more than two days in bed. I sleep well and have never lost my appetite. My trouble was laryngitis. The doctor soon cured that but before getting over it I caught a very bad cold, which affected my heart. I feel well but am very weak, gaining strength very slowly. My weakness seems due to loss of weight. In 1937, my waist was 38 inches, now it is 34.[17]

On the morning of May 3, 1940, Henry Flipper failed to appear at the family breakfast table in contrast to the clock-like military precision of his daily routine. The old solider and frontiersman was found in his bedroom, dead of heart failure at the age of eighty-four. The story of his pioneering contributions passed with him until told by historians of a later generation.

Death did not end the Flipper saga. One of the great frustrations of his life was the futile forty-year struggle he waged to reverse his court-marital conviction and gain Army reinstatement. Between 1884 and 1924, he had nine unsuccessful bills introduced in the Senate and the House of Representatives petitioning for these goals. In 1898, he had asked Booker T. Washington, America's premier black leader and spokesman, to appeal personally on his behalf to President William McKinley and to his former post commander at Fort Davis, Texas, Major General William R. Shafter.[18] In 1922, while Flipper was serving on his staff, Secretary of the Interior Albert B. Fall used his influence with Secretary of War John W. Weeks in a fruitless effort to aid Flipper's cause.[19]

In 1976, after a campaign by civil rights advocates led by Ray O. McColl, a Georgia school teacher, Flipper won a partial posthumous vindication. The Army Board of Corrections for Military Records declared that it lacked authority to reverse Flipper's conviction. It did convert his separation record to a certificate of honorable discharge, however. In 1978, his remains were moved from Atlanta to his birthplace of Thomasvillle, Georgia, and buried with full military honors.

Culturally, Henry Flipper was the type of individual that modern sociologists have characterized as a "marginal man." He rejected the limitations of the black society of his time. He could never be fully accepted in leadership positions in white society, however. Albert B. Fall described Flipper's social dilemma with perfect clarity in a 1922 letter to Senator James W. Wadsworth, Jr., chairman of the U.S. Senate Military Affairs Committee:

> His life is a most pathetic one. By education, by experience and because of his natural high intellectual characteristics, he can find no pleasure in association with many of his own race, and because of his color he was and is precluded in this country from enjoying the society of those whom he would be mentally and otherwise best fitted to associate with.[20]

Despite the near heart-breaking outcome of his military career, Flipper found at least a partial refuge from discrimination by remaining on the border frontier, with its multi-ethnic culture, where a man's practical contributions to the developing society could overcome sometimes the barriers of racial, ethnic, or national origin. On the frontier, he was able to carve out a civilian career, which would have been denied him in the supposedly more civilized regions of the America of his day.

Henry Flipper was a cultural trailblazer, and he truly earned the title of "Black Frontiersman."

Chapter 1 of the present volume was first edited and published in 1963 at El Paso, Texas, by the Texas Western College Press under the title *Negro Frontiersman*. The present edition is a reprint of the 1963 text but with numerous additional explanatory notes.

In the 1916 frontier memoirs, even the usually meticulous Flipper committed an occasional minor inconsistency in usage. An example is the use of both "Tenth" and "10th" in designating his cavalry regiment. In such cases this editor chose to retain the author's original usage. In a few instances in the 1963 edition, paragraphs were inadvertantly omitted. They have now been put in place.

1

THE WESTERN MEMOIRS

[Henry Flipper's narrative was originally a manuscript written in 1916 at El Paso, Texas. It was intended for a Mrs. Brown, an African American lady of Augusta, Georgia. She and Flipper had been close platonic friends for over thirty-five years.[1] After Flipper's death, the manuscript was donated by relatives to the Atlanta University Library and was discovered by this editor in 1960.]

I think I wrote you fully of my first experiences in the Army after I joined,[2] how I was sent to the Wichita Indian Agency to inspect and receive cattle for issue to Indians, how from ignorance of conditions and a certain amount of fear, I rode 32 miles in four hours with my white soldier orderly, how I was given the only vacant room in a combination of frontier saloon and hotel and my orderly a place in a grain room in the stable, how it stormed that night and grew intensely cold, how the cowboys came in the night with the cattle and were put in the dinning room to sleep on the floor, how they raved and swore when they knew a "nigger officer" was there to inspect and receive the cattle and was occupying the only bed, how I got up, dressed and went out and brought my orderly into the room and made him spread his blankets on the floor alongside of my bed, how I inspected the cattle next day and then rode back to Fort Sill in four hours, in the snow and cold, how my cook, Mrs. Matthews, had to cut my cowhide boots from my feet, how stiff and sore I was and how quickly I got a bath and went to bed. I was sent again to the Agency for the same purpose, but my shyness and greenness had disappeared and my confidence had reasserted itself.

I recall an amusing incident that occurred there on one occasion. There was an Indian trading store there and on this particular visit I saw a government scout and interpreter by the name of Ben Clark standing in front of the store and went over to salute him. There were two or three other white men there and a number of Indians. They were talking of the total eclipse of the sun then about due. Clark told the Indians he could put out the sun and make it dark. They did not believe him, of course. He got up on a barrel and began to wave his arms and mumble till, sure enough, the eclipse began. He kept this up till the eclipse was total, the chickens began to hunt their roosts, and the roosters began to crow lustily. The Indians looked on stoically muttering among themselves and, before any one could foresee what was going to happen, they threw themselves on to Clark and would have killed him if we had not jerked him down and shoved him in the store and closed the door. The Indians were furious. We calmed them down and told them if they would let Clark alone, he would bring the sun back and leave it. To this they agreed, Clark came out, got up on the barrel again, went through his mummery, the eclipse passed and the sun shone as brightly as ever.[3] After that the Indians never had much use for Clark, though he had been a favorite with them and had one of their squaws for a wife. He was "bad medicine" after that.[4]

I had gone to Fort Sill ahead of my Troop, which did not arrive for some time afterwards from Texas where it had been stationed. As soon as they arrived, I was made Post Signal Officer and instructed the troops there in military signalling. There were two companies of white Infantry and two troops of colored Cavalry. Do you know the difference? A company of Infantry or foot soldiers is called a *Company*, a company of Cavalry or mounted soldiers is called a *Troop*, and a company of Artillery is called a *Battery*, with four or six guns according to the kind of guns.

My Captain was a widower with a son and a daughter, both small.[5] As soon as the Troop was established in quarters, he went to San Antonio, Texas, and married a Miss Annie Dwyer. He was over fifty and she barely twenty-one. He brought her back and also her sister,

Miss Mollie Dwyer.[6] They were all Irish all through. As soon as they were settled, Mrs. Nolan insisted that I should board with them. I discharged my cook and did so. Miss Dwyer and I became fast friends and used to go horseback riding together. On Sunday we and other officers and their ladies used to chase coyotes and jackrabbits on the plains. It was great sport, something like fox chasing in England. There were great flocks of greyhounds in the Post and they had been trained to catch the coyotes and kill them. The coyote is the prairie wolf, very common in the West.

I was sent out once to guard a lot of Indian prisoners cutting rails to fence an Indian farm. There were other troops at the farm trying to teach Mr. "Lo" how to farm but it was a failure.[7] They planted potatoes once and dug them up next morning and ate them.

At another time the Post Adjutant, an Infantry officer whose name I have forgotten—O, yes, Lt. S. R. Whitall—was sent out to this farm to arrest an Indian for something he had done.[8] The Lieutenant was a mean, brutal, overbearing fellow and the Indians fired on him and he failed to get his man. I was sent out the next night with ten men in a covered wagon to get him. I went near their camp, got out and went up to their camp fire alone and unarmed. I had by that time learned a little of the Indian sign language. I joked with them, finally told them my mission and they consented to my taking the man if I would let two friends go with him. When I rode up to the Adjutant's office next morning with my prisoner, that official was dumbfounded, surly and discourteous. He did not like me anyway.

Gen. [J. W.] Davidson once issued orders that no one should walk on the grass when crossing the parade ground, but no one paid much attention to it.[9] He repeated the order one day when I happened to be Officer of the Day, sent for me, told me to put a sentinel on the parade ground with orders to arrest anybody, officer, civilian, soldier, man, woman or child, who walked on the grass. About 11 o'clock the corporal of the guard came to my quarters and told me I was wanted at the guard house at once. I rushed over there and found the sentinel had arrested the General's son, a boy 18 or 19 years old, and put him in the guard house. He wanted me to release him but I told him I could not do that. He had sent word to his mother also and while we were talking the General's orderly came with orders for me to report at once to the General's quarters. I hadn't more than stepped on the porch when I saw I was in the middle of a family row. As soon as Mrs. Davidson saw me, she yelled rather than spoke: "I want you to let my boy out of that guard house at once." And the General: "You keep him there till I order his release. I'll teach him a lesson." Mrs. Davidson kept yelling at me to release him till the General said to her: "Madam, I'll have you to know I'm the Commanding Officer of this Post." "And," she replied, "I'll have you to understand I'm your commanding officer," and a great deal more. The upshot of it all was that I was ordered to release the young man.

The First Lieutenant of my Troop was a man by the name of [R. J.] Pratt. He it was who founded the Carlyle [sic] school for Indians and was its superintendent for many years.[10] Gen. Sherman at one time ordered all officers on detached service to join their regiments and Pratt had to return. He joined us at Fort Sill. Captain Nolan had told me that he was the ugliest man the Creator had ever fashioned out of clay. One afternoon, at stables—when the horses are groomed and fed—Captain Nolan and I were walking up and down the picket line while the men were grooming the horses. He had told me that Pratt was expected in the stage that day. As we turned at the end of the line to walk back, whom should we see but Lieutenant Pratt coming toward us. He was a tall, lean, lank, raw-boned specimen. He wore a long, loose linen duster reaching nearly to his feet and flapping in the breeze. As he got near us and before he could speak, Captain Nolan said, so that all the men could hear: "God damn it, Mr. Pratt, leave the picket line; you'll stampede my horses!" All officers always addressed juniors by "Mr." and superiors by their military title.

Fort Sill was situated on a high plateau at the junction of two streams, Cache Creek and Medicine Bluff Creek, had the best water in the world and ought to have been very, very healthy, but it was not. I got my system full of malaria at Fort Sill, but of this more anon. There was a series of shallow ponds extending from Fort Sill to Red

"Black Jack" Davidson, Flipper's commanding officer at Fort Sill (repro-duced from Homer K. Davidson, Black Jack Davidson: A Cavalry Commander on the Western Frontier. . . . *Courtesy of the Arthur H. Clark Company).*

River, more than 40 miles. They filled up in the rainy season and remained stagnant most of the year. There was much malaria in the Post and many soldiers died of it.

[One time] when the ponds were dry and before the rains set in, General Davidson detailed me to dig a ditch and drain them. He gave me a full Troop of Cavalry and I went down, made my surveys and estimates and came back and reported to him. He then ordered a Troop of Cavalry to report to me every Sunday morning, relieving the one that had worked the week before. I finished the ditch and the Commanding Officer and other officers went down to look it over. We got down in the ditch and the General told me I had it running up hill and that the grade was wrong. It certainly looked that way, but I knew I was right. You stand on a level street and look along it and it seems to rise and grow narrower, although you know it is of uniform width and level. However, I put the instrument on it and convinced him it was all right. When the rains came, the water flowed away perfectly and there never were any more ponds. The health of the Post improved wonderfully. I have been told the ditch is still there and is known as "Flipper's Ditch."[11]

On one occasion the Indian Agent gave a large bunch of Indians permission to go hunting without notifying the Commanding Officer, who was furious. The military was responsible for the conduct of the Indians, had to protect them and also the settlers scattered about the country. Whenever they went out without escort they always slipped over into Texas, stole horses and cattle and even killed people. Gen. Davidson ordered Captain Nolan to take his whole Troop, overhaul these Indians and keep with them while they were hunting. As Captain Nolan could not get started in less than half a day, I was ordered to take ten men, select horses, and ride hard till I overtook them and then to hold them where I found them till the Troop came up. We started at daybreak after a hasty breakfast and rode all day, not even stopping for lunch, and overhauled them late that night. We camped with them and when we unpacked our animals, we found we had no rations. The Sergeant had forgotten to load them on the mules. The Indians had been unable to do any hunting on account of the heavy snow and cold. When we overtook them they had just killed a horse and were roasting the meat over the coals. We had to eat horse meat for two days till the Troop arrived.

Every fall the Indian Agent let contracts for cutting wood and mild hay for the Indians through the winter and the contractors were always Texans, who came up for the purpose and camped on the Reservation. In previous years when they went home they always stole and drove off large herds of Indian ponies. When the end of the contract in question came, I was sent to the Agency, with a full Troop, to take charge of them and escort them to the Texas line. As fast as they were paid I took charge of them and next day took them down and put them over the line into Texas.

The Commanding Officer at Fort Sill received word from a Texas company of Rangers that they had discovered a large lake on the Staked Plains and I was sent to investigate and report. The Staked Plains of Texas are large, high, flat plateaus in Northwest Texas and get their name from this circumstance. The early Catholic priests and monks went over them in the 16th century carrying the Gospel to the Indians, and, in order not to get lost, drove stakes in the ground as they went along so as to guide them on their return journey.

I left Fort Sill in November with twenty men and two wagons and a guide. On the march we camped at a place called Tepee City which consisted of one dugout and one family. A dugout is one room scooped out of an embankment with dirt floor and roof and three dirt sides, a hole in the roof for the smoke to escape and a piece of canvas, brush, or anything handy in front. Before our supper a white man came up and wanted to know who was in command. I was pointed out to him, he came up, introduced himself and wanted me to administer the oath of office to his wife who had been appointed postmistress at Tepee City. I was amazed and protested that I had no authority to do such a thing. They were from Kansas, had come down there, taken up a piece of land and she had been appointed postmistress. He said his wife was in a condition that precluded her riding more than a hundred miles to Fort Worth to be sworn in and that the papers themselves stated that any Army officer might administer the oath where there were no civil officers. He invited me to his dugout to see the papers and to supper. I was glad to go for the supper, glad for something different from fried bacon and soldier bread. We had fried venison with bacon, coffee with cream, milk, butter they had made, and some fruit, all well prepared. The wife could hardly walk around let alone riding horseback to Fort Worth. After supper I looked the papers over by the light of a tallow candle and administered the oath of office to her. They were tickled to death. The mail rider from Fort Worth to Fort Elliott passed there once a week, so they had an opportunity to mail the document to Washington.

Do you know what soldier bread is? Flour is mixed with salt and water into a rather stiff dough. It is then put into a Dutch oven till about an inch thick. Water is then poured in until about an inch deep. The lid is put on and a hot fire is maintained under and over the oven till the water is all converted into steam and the bread completely serrated [sic]. When hot and freshly made it is good and very palatable, but when it gets cold, it falls and becomes hard and soggy and a mule can't eat it. In those days baking powder was almost unknown on the plains and yeast could not be used in camp. There were no real cooks. Any soldier was detailed as a cook, whether he knew anything about it or not. Nowadays there are trained cooks and Army bread is as good as the best.

We found the lake. It was merely a depression that had been filled by rains. There was no water on the plains except in two or three places and not there all the time.

I was on the plains another time with Captain Nolan with the whole Troop. We divided the command. I was to go to one water hole and he to another. If I found water, I was to remain there till he returned. If not, I was to follow him. I was either to join him before he turned back or to meet him coming back. I found no water and went on. We were forty-eight hours without water for man or beast, but luckily we had lots of canned tomatoes, so that we did not suffer. Three years before, Captain Nolan had been on the plains and had had twenty-two men die from thirst and lost a lot of horses, so that he was very uneasy on this trip. It was summer time and we travelled at night by moonlight on account of the heat. Captain Nolan was moon-blind. I rode at the head of the column and he rode by my side with his leg just behind and touching mine. He couldn't see a thing by moonlight.

On this trip we went into Fort Concho to get supplies, as we had been out for four months. We camped near the Post and there was a constant stream of colored women, officers' servants, soldiers' wives, etc., to see the colored officer. I was a veritable curiosity. One day Lt. Wallace McTear of the 24th Infantry came down and said he had been sent by the officers of the Post to invite me to a dinner to be given in my honor and gave me the day and hour.[12] The next day he came down and apologized and said the Commanding Officer had forbidden the dinner and it was off. The Commanding Officer was Major Anson Mills of my own regiment, a native born Texan. This [El Paso] is his home. He owns a twelve-story office building here and once in a banquet here spoke of me very kindly indeed.[13] I dined, however, several times with Lt. [C.R.] Ward of my regiment.[14] More of this later.

On another occasion, when I was Officer of the Day, General Davidson sent his orderly for me about midnight. This was at Fort Sill. I went at once and he said to me: "Mr. Flipper, I know the men are gambling but I can't catch them at it and every officer in the Post has failed. I want you to see if you can catch any of them. Go all over the garrison, in and around the barracks, back of officers' quarters and if you see lights in the servants' quarters, go in and arrest any soldier you find or anybody else who is gambling and report to me." The old man used to prowl around the Post at all hours of the night. I went all over the garrison and around the barracks and officers' and servants' quarters and found nothing. It occurred to me to visit the barracks again. I was just leaving the last one when I heard a noise as of some one shuffling his feet. It came from overhead and when I looked up I saw a light shining through the tiniest crack. I went out and got a guard and came back and found fifteen or twenty men gambling in the garret. They had loosened a plank or two in the ceiling and could push up with a light ladder turning these planks over. Then they would climb up, pull the ladder up and turn the planks down into place and gamble most of the night, almost perfectly secure from detection. The General was tickled to death when I reported to him and chuckled with glee. [One night] I caught some men gambling in the room of an officer's servant. They ran for the barracks and beat me to them. When I entered every bed was occupied, every man was asleep and snoring. Of course, if I had turned the bedding back, I would have found my men, but I did not disturb them.

One [day] hostile Indians came into Fort Sill, cut our horses from the picket line and drove them off in broad daylight. [Later] about 2,000 of them came to the Post and had a war dance around the flag pole on the parade ground. They were starving and demanded food. The Commanding Officer wired Washington and got permission to issue rations to them, when they went away satisfied.

Another time a big crowd of Indians rushed into the Post, whooping and yelling after another [Indian] who ran into the office of the Commanding Officer. They had caught one of their squaws in the carnal sin and were going to cut off both of her ears and drive her out of the camp and tribe, as was their custom. She fled to the Post for safety where she got it.

At one [point] "G" Troop of my regiment had no officers. Captain Phil L. Lee was under arrest for something at Fort Leavenworth, I think. First Lt. [S.R.] Colladay was absent on sick leave and the Troop had no Second Lieutenant.[15] I was detailed to command the Troop as acting Captain and did so for four or five months till Captain Lee returned. Captain Lee was a cousin of Gen. Robert E. Lee, but had served in the Union Army all through the civil war and was a warm friend of mine.[16] We frequently exchanged visits.

Fort Sill was 115 miles from the railroad at Caddo station. All freight for the government was hauled over this road which was bad for many reasons. A man in Little Rock, Arkansas, got the contract for freighting and he interested himself in getting a better road and a shorter one. It was decided to build a road from Fort Sill to the same railroad but to another station of more importance and over a shorter route. A lieutenant and a Troop of the 4th Cavalry were sent out to build the road. He reached Gainesville, Texas, where most of his men got drunk; many deserted and left him in the middle of a bad fix. He was compelled to return to the Post and get a good reprimand. I was then sent out with my Troop to build the road. I went all the way through Gainesville carefully selecting and marking my route. We were cordially received in Gainesville by the white people who were anxious to have the road put through. I was there two or three days getting things in shape and during that time they sent us all sorts of nice things to eat. Starting back, I constructed the road and when we reached home it was finished. The Arkansas man who had the freighting contract was notified just before I finished and he came down and rode over the road in a light buggy to test it. He was very much pleased and with the first freight wagon that came out he sent me a huge barrel filled with all sorts of fine liquors, old whiskeys, brandies, wines, and cigars. At the time I never touched any of those things and gave them all away to friends among the officers. They all said they were the best that money could buy. That country is all settled now, is Oklahoma, and that road is still in use, very much improved of course and kept in good order.

In the fall of 1879, we were ordered to proceed to Fort Elliott, Texas, and take station. When the Troop left Fort Sill I had to remain behind an hour or so for some purpose. Finally I started alone. The road as it leaves Fort Sill climbs a hill. When I reached the top of the hill, I stopped, turned around and looked back over Fort Sill and, would you believe it? I wept like a child, the last time in my life I have ever found it possible to weep. Now I am easily moved by anything that is tender, a brave act or something of that kind and tears will run down my cheek, but there on that hill, I wept like a child. I hated to leave Fort Sill. A year afterwards we marched through there on our way to the Rio Grande and I have not seen Fort Sill since.

At Fort Elliott, up in the Panhandle of Texas, my Captain, Capt. Nolan, was the senior officer present and therefore the Commanding Officer. I was made Post Adjutant. The Post Adjutant is the executive officer. All business is transacted through him. He receives and opens all official mail and all mail goes through him. If any one wants anything, he must go to the Adjutant. He is the ranking officer on the Commanding Officer's staff. There was one Troop of the 4th Cavalry, white, one of the 10th Cavalry, Colored, and two companies of the 23rd Infantry, white.

Several murders had been committed at Fort Elliott and it was not certain whether they were on or off the military reservation. I was detailed to survey and make a map of the reservation, which I did.

[When] a large amount of ammunition was stolen from the ordnance room and we could not get a clew to the thief, I was sent with a dozen men to a little town way up on the New Mexico border called Tascosa.[17] It was then a sheep and cattle country and the inhabitants were mostly Mexicans. I reached there on a Sunday morning and the place was full of cowboys and shepherds, Mexicans and Americans, and I was very uncertain how to proceed, but I finally searched every house in the place and then went to the only store kept by a man by the name of McMasters. I put a guard around the house and then went in with my Sergeant at my heels, all of us fully armed. I told Mr. McMasters what my mission was and that I wanted to search his store. To my surprise he told me to go ahead. I and the Sergeant searched every nook in the house and found a small back room literally covered with the paper packages in which the ammunition comes packed but not a single cartridge. I asked Mr. McMasters how they came there, but he would give me no satisfactory explanation. I took a gunny sack of these papers and returned to Fort Elliott and reported.

The matter was reported to the U.S. Marshal at Fort Worth, Texas. He came up, made an investigation, went to Tascosa and returned with two men, one of them the mail rider. I happened to be Officer of the Day. He went to the guard house and wanted to keep his prisoners there over night and the Sergeant of the guard sent for me. I refused to receive them without an order from the Commanding Officer. He saw the C.O., came back and said I was to receive them. I refused to do so without a written order, which he went and got, and then I held his prisoners over night for him. We discovered that the Quartermaster Sergeant, in charge of this property, had been stealing it and selling it to cowboys, sending it up through the country by mail rider. He was sent to Leavenworth military prison for three years. His friends burnt down the office of the C.O. one night hoping to destroy the record of the court martial, but fortunately the Adjutant had taken it to his quarters to read it over at his leisure and thus saved it.

When the marshal reached Fort Worth with his prisoners, he reported to the U. S. grand jury and both Captain Nolan and myself were indicted for violating the Posse Comitatus act of 1878, which forbade the use of the Army for arresting or holding civilians. A firm of lawyers in Fort Worth wrote us offering to defend us, told us not to go to Fort Worth then, as the cases would not be called till the next term, that they had arranged bonds, etc. When the next term arrived I received a telegram to be on hand. I got a leave of absence and started. When I reached the railroad at Caddo, Indian Territory, there was a telegram telling me not to go and I returned to Fort Sill. Captain Nolan happened to be in that neighborhood buying horses for the government. He went to Fort Worth, appeared before the court, pleaded guilty and was fined one dollar. He asked that the same plea be entered for me and the same fine against me. This was done and he paid the two dollars. So you see [I have] been a criminal, deep dyed in crime of the most heinous kind.

At Fort Elliott, Captain [Clarence] Mauck, "B" Troop, 4th Cavalry, was retired and Lt. [H.W.] Lawton was promoted to Captain in his place. Lawton was 1st Lieutenant and Regimental Quartermaster of the 4th Cavalry and Post Quartermaster at Fort Sill when I joined, helped me select my quarters and furnished them from the quartermaster's department. The first night he spent in Elliott, he sent for me and Lt. [T.M.] Wenie of the 23rd Infantry, white. He had previously sent to the Post Trader's and had got a barrel of beer, beer in bottles. Well—close your eyes and put your fingers in your ears—we three drank that barrel of beer before we quit; the first, last, and only time I ever drank beer. Of course I wasted all I could and drank as little as I could and drank because of my great admiration for Lawton. He was a giant in size and one of the most powerful men I ever saw. I met him years afterwards at Santa Fe when he was Inspector General and was in his quarters one night. He, myself, and Lt. Harrison of his staff were present. Lawton was full, Harrison said something that did not please him and he grabbed at the mantel piece, yanked it from the wall and tossed it at Lt. Harrison who saved himself by dodging out of the door.[18]

At early day light I sent for my horse and rode out in the crisp morning air ten, twelve, fifteen miles and back, and then a bath and I was all right again. I had a dun Andalusian stallion I bought from Captain Mauck for $200, a magnificent animal, the only stallion in the regiment and as gentle as a cat. Miss Mollie Dwyer was crazy to ride him but I declined with one pretext and another, because I was afraid he might hurt her. She finally rode him out to my camp once, riding nine miles in fifty-five minutes.

About this time Lt.-Col. John W. Hatch of the 4th Cavalry came to Fort Elliott as Commanding Officer and the first night he was there the officers called in a body to pay their respects. He was an old man, had been a General in the civil war. He entertained us till late in the night recounting his Army experiences. I remember he told us he had not finished paying off debts contracted while a cadet at West Point and that he had not been on a horse in twenty years, although he was a Lt.-Col. of Cavalry.[19]

[Soon] I was detailed to build a telegraph line from Fort Elliott, Texas, to Fort Supply, Indian Territory. Lt. [J.A.] Swift of the Signal Corps was in charge of the work.[20] He had contractors cut the poles and distribute them, as also the wire, and all I was supposed to do was to put it up. The first two or three days I found there were not more than half enough poles and had to snake poles back, leaving big gaps without poles. He complained to the Commanding Officer about the slow progress I was making and I was called in to explain, which I did. I persuaded him to let me cut poles, any kind of old poles, as I went along just to get the line up, as we could put in poles of the proper length and kind afterwards. Lt. Swift had a brand new wife in Washington and he was anxious to get back to her. What a baleful influence women have over us poor men, helpless creatures that we are! It's awful! Under this arrangement I put up over nine miles of wire in one day, much to his satisfaction. It was to one of my camps on this work that Miss Dwyer rode out on my stallion, nine miles in fifty-five minutes. Wonderful riding for a woman!

Mrs. Lt. [J. A.] Maney of the 23rd Infantry, white, gave a birthday party at her quarters and sent me an invitation.[21] I did not go because I thought it was only a courtesy invitation. I went to bed early, but Lt. and Mrs. Maney came to my quarters, roused me out and wanted to know why I had not gone to her party. She did not wait for excuses but told me they would not leave the door till I got up, dressed, and went back with them, which I had to do. When we reached the house, they were dancing some round dance and she wanted me to get right into it with her, but I could not. It was beyond me. The next was a square dance. She came and got me and against my protest made me go through the motions with her and I had to dance every square dance after that with her or some other lady till the dancing ended.

I had a most peculiar experience one night at Elliott. I was Officer of the Day and, as I had to inspect the guard at least once between midnight and day light, I retired early. Early in the night I was awakened by what I thought, what I knew, was the fire call which the bugler was sounding. Wide awake, I jumped out of bed, dressed rapidly, buckled on my saber and rushed out on the front porch. There I stopped awe-struck. It was the most beautiful moonlight night I ever saw any where. There wasn't a light any where, not a person astir, not a sound any where. If a pin had dropped out in the grass on the parade ground, I would have heard it. I was impressed with the profound calmness, tranquility, beauty, and peacefulness of the night. I stood there many moments and enjoyed it. Of course, the fire call had not sounded. Probably dreaming, my subconscious mind took in the notes of taps, the call to extinguish lights, sounded every night in military garrisons. I had gone to bed before the time for taps and when it sounded was doubtless dreaming and confounded the two calls. Taps and fire call are very much alike. I surely enjoyed the impression made on me, in which the dominant feature was Peace.

In the spring of 1880 our Troop and two others at Fort Sill were ordered to Fort Davis, Texas, for station and to go into the campaign at once against Victorio and his band of hostile Mescalero Apaches, who were on the war path in New Mexico, southwest Texas and northern Mexico. We had to march over 1,200 miles. Before reaching the Red River we came to a very deep creek that was flooded and we could not cross. We waited two or three days for the water to go down but it kept raining and the creek showed no signs of falling. I suggested to the Captain a way to get over and, after I explained it to him, he told me to go ahead. I had all the wagons unloaded, took the body from one and wrapped a tent fly around it, making a boat of it. I then had a man swim across with a rope, each end of which he tied securely to a tree. In this way I rigged up a ferry on which we ferried over all our effects, the women and children and then swam the horses and mules. We then put the wagons together and pursued our journey. I expected to have to do the same thing at the Red River. It was high also, but it was very wide and shallow and was no obstacle.

We proceeded on our way and finally reached Fort Davis, then commanded by Major N. B. McLaughlin of my regiment, a very fine officer and gentleman.[22] We remained there just long enough to get our quarters arranged and were ordered into the field against the Indians. They had broken out in New Mexico, had committed all sorts of depredations and had been driven into Mexico by the 9th Cavalry, colored. They swung around into Texas and we were sent against them. My Troop and "G" Troop, 10th Cavalry, some of the 8th Cavalry, white, from Fort Clark, Texas, and the 9th Cavalry, were the units in the field. There was also a single company of Texas Rangers. We were ordered to old Fort Quitman, an abandoned fort on the north bank of the Rio Grande. Here I was made Camp Quartermaster and Commissary. We did considerable scouting from here. Forty miles below us on the river there was a picket of a lieutenant and ten men. The Indians surprised them one morning at day light and killed several of them, got all their equipment, horses, etc. Two of the men, in underclothing, reaching our camp in the afternoon with the news and Captain Nolan sent me and two men with dispatches to Gen. [B.H.]

Benjamin H. Grierson (Fort Davis National Historic Site).

Grierson at Eagle Springs.[23] I rode 98 miles in 22 hours mostly at night, through a country the Indians were expected to traverse in their efforts to get back to New Mexico. I had no bad effects from the hard ride till I reached the General's tent. When I attempted to dismount, I found I was stiff and sore and fell from my horse to the ground, waking the General. He wanted to know what had happened and the sentinel, who had admitted me, had to answer for me. One of the men unsaddled my horse, spread the saddle blanket on the ground, I rolled over on it and with the saddle for a pillow, slept till the sun shining in my face woke me next morning. I then rode back.

There were no troops at Eagle Springs where the General was. He was riding in an ambulance and was returning from our camp. He ordered the troops concentrated there and we started for that place. Other troops were coming from the opposite direction. The Indians attacked the General the morning after I left. He and the half dozen men of the escort with him got up in the rocks and stood them off till we could arrive, a courier having been sent by him to hurry us. We came in a swinging gallop for fifteen or twenty miles. When we arrived we found "G" Troop had already come and the fight was on. We got right into it and soon had the Indians on the run. We lost 19 horses, had two or three men killed, a number wounded, among them Lt. Colladay of "G" Troop, and got 19 Indians. We buried the soldiers where they fell. I was detailed to read the Episcopal service over them, after which a volley was fired and the buglers sounded taps. This was the first and only time I was under fire, but escaped without a scratch.

Our scouts reported that the Indians had crossed into Mexico, but two or three days afterwards we got word that they had crossed the road during the night only a little way from us and were heading for Fresno Spring. Gen. Grierson determined to get there first and started about 1 o'clock in the afternoon and rode till midnight without stopping. We got there and at once took position for a fight. No lights or fires were allowed and we had to eat cold suppers without coffee. Saddles were not removed either. If they once got in as far as the spring, we would have them surrounded and every vantage point occupied. About 11 o'clock next day they were reported entering the canyon. We had a wagon train coming from Fort Davis to Eagle Springs. It was diverted to Fresno Spring, by whose order I never knew. It hove in sight and the Indians saw it before we did and before they had seen us and with a hideous yell they rushed to attack it. We were thus compelled to leave our hiding places to protect the train and when we opened fire, the Indians turned and fled and we never saw them again although we took up the trail and followed them. They, with their women and children, gathered at a place called Tres Castillos in Mexico. While the above incidents were going on, the Mexicans surprised the camp and killed them all.[24] The warriors greatly reduced in numbers scattered and worked their way back to the reservation. We were then ordered back to our station at Fort Davis, Texas.

For services in the field I was made Acting Assistant Quartermaster and Post Quartermaster and Acting Commissary of Subsistence and Post Commissary. I had charge of the entire military reservation, houses, water and fuel supply, transportation, feed, clothing and equipment for troops and the food supply. Within a few days after my appointment, I had a letter from Lt. Ward of my regiment, who held the same position at Ford Stockton, Texas, to the effect that he was four Army wagons short and wanted to know if I had them or could help him, as otherwise he would have to pay for them. I did not have his wagons, but I had all of my own and a large number of condemned wagons that had not been destroyed because of the absence of troops from the Post. I picked out four of the best ones, had my wheelwright repair and repaint them and sent them down to him. I shall have occasion to refer to Lieut. Ward again. Don't forget him.

In February [1881], I was sitting at dinner in my quarters. I was so sitting that I could look out of a window and see my hay stacks. We had no grain in the Post for the animals. All we had and all we could buy was used in the campaign, but there was an oversupply of hay, as none had been used for the same reason. It had been snowing for several days and nights. There were eight to ten inches of snow on the ground and I was wearing my high cavalry boots, as I was on the go nearly all the time. As I looked out of the window I saw flames shoot up out of one of the largest hay ricks right through the snow. I jumped out, seized my cap and rushed out of the building and down to the stacks. The fire alarm was sounded and the troops turned out. I worked there all the afternoon and all night. Our efforts to save the stack utterly failed, as it must have been burnt out inside before the flames burst through, but we saved the other stacks, thanks to the snow on them and their damp outsides. We had no fire department but used buckets. A soldier would come up with a bucket of water. I would take it and toss it up on the stack only to have it run down off the stack all over me and into my boots and freeze. Think of working in that condition all night. Wet all over and frozen stiff. And the worry and anxiety. The stack was set afire by a white clerk I had discharged. That was the general belief, but there was no proof. I at once asked for a board of survey and it fully relieved me of all responsibility.

But two or three days afterwards I was in bed with a severe case of typhoid malarial fever and no medicines in the Post; they had all been consumed in the campaign and the requisitions had not yet arrived. Doubtless I had brought the malaria from Fort Sill and this catastrophe brought it out. The Post Surgeon and the Commanding Officer took the best of care of me. Every night Major McLaughlin sat up with me, as also did the Surgeon. One night the latter, who had been with me several hours, hunted up the Major and told him I would not live three quarters of an hour. That shows how sick I was. The Surgeon used to give me a quarter grain dose of morphine every night. I got better in spite of all and one day they took me on a stretcher to the Quartermaster's office to open the safe so the clerk could pay off my civilian employees, teamsters, packers, saddler, blacksmith, etc. I gradually got better, used to sit on the porch and finally one day called for my horse. He was brought, I mounted and started off. He hadn't been ridden all the time I was sick and I couldn't hold him. I had to call a soldier to help me down and take me home and take the horse to the stable.

There was a fence around Fort Davis, with a turnstile for people afoot and a gate for wagons. The turnstile was nearer my quarters than the gate and I never went to the gate. I just jumped the turn-stile.

Miss Dwyer and I continued our rides at Fort Davis for a short time. Lt. Pratt did not stay with us long. He was ordered back to theIndian School at Carlisle and we got a new 1st Lieutenant by the name of Charles L. Cooper. He had a wife and a daughter nearly grown [and] came from the civil war Army.[25] [They] were nice people. He was soon promoted and we got Charles E. Nordstrom as 1st Lieutenant. He also came from the civil war Army, was a Swede from Maine, had no education and was a brute.[26] He hated me and gradually won Miss Dwyer from her horse back rides with me and himself took her riding in a buggy he had. Lieut. Nordstrom and I occupied the same set of double quarters. There was a common entrance and a common hall, but otherwise our quarters were separate. He married Miss Dwyer after I was dismissed. I shall have occasion to speak of them again.

New Year's Day in 1881, the only officer who visited me was Lieut. [Wade] Hampton, a nephew of the famous confederate Gen. Wade Hampton of South Carolina.[27] The rest of the officers of the Post were hyenas. Lieut. Hampton was a splendid, nice fellow. Some years afterwards another nephew worked with me in Chihuahua as a surveyor.

In 1881, Major McLaughlin was relieved as Commanding Officer and replaced by Col. W. R. Shafter of the 1st Infantry, white. He at once relieved me as Quartermaster and informed me he would relieve me as Commissary as soon as he could find an officer for the place and then he and his Adjutant, Lieut. [Louis] Wilhelmi,[28] and Nordstrom began to persecute me and lay traps for me. I was warned by civilians and never did a man walk the path of uprightness straighter than I did, but the trap was cunningly laid and I was sacrificed, effective June 30, 1882.[29] All the men connected with that nefarious scheme are long since dead. Lieut. —— —— came in one night from some detached duty and caught his wife sitting nude on another officer's lap. Lt. —— ——'s wife went into a sporting house in Los Angeles, and he died in disgrace. Lt. —— —— died at Santa Fe, leaving his wife and two daughters in dire poverty; and [another officer's] only daughter was ruined by a private soldier. There has

William R. Shafter, Flipper's accuser at Fort Davis. Below, Fort Davis. In the foreground is the guardhouse where Flipper was housed during the court-martial (both photos courtesy Fort Davis National Historic Site).

surely been retributive justice in my case. Every man that participated in the case against me, including the members of the court-martial, are all dead.[30]

When my dismissal became effective I sold my horses—I had three—to Lieut. Nordstrom and my other effects to civilians. Among my effects was an Army tent I had bought when I entered the service, my name was on it and I had always used it. Every officer and man in the regiment knew it was my private property. Even Nordstrom did not object to my selling it to a civilian. After I had left, Lieut. Ward came along, saw the tent and seized it as government property, claiming that I had stolen it and had no right to sell it. The civilian came back on me and I had to refund him his money. . . .

After leaving the Army in 1882, I came to El Paso. I did nothing special worth mentioning till the fall of 1883.[31] In that year the Mexican government began to give concessions for surveying public lands. The concessionaires received one third of the public lands surveyed. A Mexican company of Chihuahua obtained a concession covering the State of that name and transferred it to an American company, which was to do the work, the resulting land to be divided between the companies or all sold to the American company. This latter was composed entirely of ex-Confederate officers, Gen. Harrison, Major Kneeland, Major Zimpleman, Captain Beall and others. They engaged as engineer a man by the name of A. Q. Wingo, who had been a private in the 1st Arkansas Cavalry, of which his father was Colonel, also in the southern Army. I knew Wingo, having met him surveying in various parts of Texas when I was scouting with the Army. Wingo went down, looked the situation over and wrote the company to send him an assistant at once and named me. I was employed but before I could go, I was notified there was some objection because of my race. They wrote their objections to Wingo and proposed another man, a white man. Wingo told them to send me or send a man to take his place. I was hurried down to him without any more ado.

I found Chihuahua, a town of about 22,000 inhabitants, without a single hotel or restaurant. Wingo was in what they call a *meson* (may-sóne) and what we would call a wagon yard. There were stables for horses, etc., a yard for wagons and rooms without furniture of any kind. You had to furnish your own bedding and sleep on the floor. As we had to camp out in our survey work, we bought our bedding. To live we had to find a woman to cook for us in her own house and we would give her every morning enough money to buy the food for the day. After we had received instructions and been officially appointed surveyors, we went to Santa Rosalia, some 40 miles south of Chihuahua, and there organized our party, engaged a cook, helpers, got two four-mule wagons, bought provisions and got ready to proceed to work.

I was in a new world. I spoke Spanish fairly well. There was but one school in Chihuahua and that was for boys, girls not being deemed worthy of learning anything, beyond enough to read the prayer book, when they learned anything at all. The teacher was a pathetic priest and the pupils studied aloud, as they do to this day. No young girl ever went out on the street without a relative or a *dueña*, generally some old hag who never hesitated to sell her young charge at any time, as was often done. On Sundays the people gathered in the *plaza* (park) and promenaded, the men going one way and the women the opposite way. You never saw a couple together unless they were husband and wife. The people were intensely Catholic, externally, and were in the churches all the time. When a man passed in front of a church, he took his hat off. With all that the people were and are the most immoral I ever saw. There was a street called the Street of the 11,000 virgins, given wholly over to the unregenerated Magdalenes. Gambling was common. With the advent of the railroad in 1882, the Protestants began to organize churches and schools and met with all sorts of obstacles. Mr. Eaten, a P. E. minister, rented a large house in which to hold services and as soon as the woman who owned it learned what his purpose was, she tried to get him out, offered to return the money, offered to double it and failing, went to the governor and the courts, but these latter refused to interfere. As always happens the women are more religious apparently than the men. Now, there are a P.E. church, a Methodist church South, and a

Baptist church in Chihuahua, each with its school. There is also a German Lutheran church and school and a Y.M.C.A. Americans have also established hotels, and there are hotels and rooming houses run by Americans, Germans, Italians, French, and Spaniards and restaurants without end of all grades and classes. There are Chinese and a few Negroes.

Once we had our party organized, in November, 1883, we left Santa Rosalia for our field of operations. I forgot to say there were four kinds of money—American money, Mexican silver, Mexican copper and Mexican paper and all had a different value. There were dollars, half dollars, quarters, *reales* (12 ½ cents), *medios* (6 ¼ cents), and the coppers called *tlacos* (64 to the dollar). It was very confusing in buying anything. For instance: What is this worth? *Real, medio y tlaco.* If you had the three coins, it was easy, but if you gave a quarter, you had to figure the change. It was simply impossible for a gringo. Now 1 *real* is 8 *tlacos*; 1 *medio* is four *tlacos* and 1 *tlaco* makes 13 *tlacos*. A quarter is 16 *tlacos*, so there were 3 *tlacos* change or 4¹¹⁄₁₆ cents. Can you figure it out?

We paid $32 for a 12-inch Dutch oven. We asked the price of sugar in a store and were asked how much we wanted. A single pound was so much. If we wanted 25 pounds or more, the price would be higher. Just think of raising the price when selling by wholesale. This reminds me of an incident that occurred years afterwards in Ocampo. A Mexican merchant got in a shipment of extra good American shoes and the Americans bought them like hot cakes. Some who missed the chance asked this merchant why he did not get more of those shoes. With a shrug of the shoulder and a forlorn gesture with both hands, he exclaimed: "What's the use? I can't keep them."

Well, we drove out of Santa Rosalia over a country as flat as your parlor floor and as dry as a burning coal and reached a small lake where Mexicans were making salt by evaporating the salt water, and we camped for the night. It snowed on us during the night, but we pulled out next morning and camped early on the desert. Our men couldn't stand it any longer; they were freezing. They had no clothes other than "*calzón blanco y huaraches,*" that is trousers and shirts made of unbleached muslin and rawhide sandals under the soles of their feet and one little cotton blanket each, in which they slept at night and used as a shawl or overcoat during the day. There was not a chip of wood any where nor a drop of water, but we knew we could melt the snow. On the Western prairies there is a bush that stands a foot or so above the ground called mesquite. If you dig down, you will almost invariably find a large root, often as big as a man's body. The roots go down for water in this dry country and that is why they grow so big below and so little above ground. This was the wood used at Forts Davis and Stockton and it was bought and sold by weight. It is exceedingly heavy and burns like coal. Wingo and I took an ax each and went out to hunt wood. You can imagine our task, as there was a foot of snow at least on the level and these little bushes were covered up. We walked and walked but found no mesquite. Finally we got into a depression or wet weather creek and found four or five big logs, trunks of trees that had been brought down by the water we knew not from where nor when, probably from the distant mountains. We lost no time in getting into them and found they were black walnut. We cut and split a quantity and started back to camp with as much as we could carry. It was more than a mile away but we got back and made a huge fire to thaw out our Mexicans. After resting we went back and got more and cooked supper. Next morning we took a wagon and brought in a good big load. We remained there three or four days till the weather cleared and proceeded to work.

On this trip we found a Spaniard on the desert dying from thirst. We revived him and took him into a settlement, where he got a guide to take him to Chihuahua. He had been prospecting in the mountains, had missed the road and watering places on the desert and was actually dying from thirst.

We ran the line between the States of Chihuahua and Coahuila and reached the Rio Grande on Christmas Day, 1883, practically out of food but with plenty of money and no where to buy anything. For supper and breakfast we had *sopaipillas*. Can you pronounce it? It is So-py-pé-yas. We had nothing but a little flour and *panocha* (pah-nó-chah), a sort of crude, dark brown sugar in cakes resembling maple sugar. A rather stiff dough is made of flour and water. Balls of this are taken and worked out in the hand to about 18 inches in diameter and about as thick as this sheet of paper and held before the fire and cooked. A great stack of them is made. Then a rather thin syrup is made from the *panocha* and the bread is soaked in it. They are good. They are used by Mexicans at religious feasts such as Christmas eve which they celebrate instead of Christmas. Nor do they give Christmas gifts as we do. I must tell you about that. Ten families agree to have the celebration. On the ninth day preceding Christmas eve, one of these families visits another of the ten and asks for lodging and so on till Christmas eve. They are always refused, sometimes a servant is called and they are led off the premises to the street. Each succeeding night they tell a pitiful story of how they have vainly sought lodging and have been refused. On Christmas eve night they reach the house where the celebration is to be had and there after listening to their story, they are kindly received and invited in, where they find the other families assembled and any other invited guests. There is usually a supper and dancing. At a certain hour in the evening they have what they call the *piñata* (peen-yáh-tah). This is a large, fragile, earthen pot made for the purpose. It is previously filled with candy, bonbons and other things dear to the heart of the Mexican child and hung in the middle of the parlor. Some person is selected to break it, usually a young girl. She is carefully blindfolded, given a long pole and turned loose to find the *piñata* and break it. Of course, they try to keep her away from it, some telling her it is here and some there, till she finally finds it and with a good blow breaks it. The candies and other things fall all over the floor and the children and young people have lots of fun scrambling for it.

Having reached the river and had our *sopaipillas*, we crossed over to inspect what appeared to be the ruins of a house. The door was closed but not fastened. We entered and found it full of corn, pumpkins, and other things, among them some dried venison. We had not seen a human being for many days, but we helped ourselves to pumpkins and venison. Our work finished, we turned toward home by a shorter route and some thirty miles from the river ran into a small settlement called Santa Rosa. There was no store there, no farming and we wondered how the people lived. We learned that they farmed on the American side in season at the house we had visited but lived mainly by smuggling. They were a hard looking set and we did not remain there very long.

In due time we reached a town called Meoqui of some importance on the new railroad, rented a house and prepared to make our maps. We had not more than got our things in the house before I was arrested and thrown into a filthy Mexican jail. Mr. Wingo telegraphed the manager in Chihuahua and he saw the governor, who was a stockholder in the company.[32] He wired the authorities and I was released and that was the end of it. I did not know why I had been arrested till later. I had a friend in El Paso by the name of Bainbridge, a barber. We corresponded occasionally and in a letter I mentioned something I had heard and afterwards had fully confirmed. It was to the effect that a priest was living openly with his daughter and had two or three children by her. This priest was a near connection of a leading family in Chihuahua and the richest in Mexico. They are living here in El Paso now, refugees from their own country and cannot return, because they are rich.[33] Bainbridge showed the letter to the editor of the *Lone Star*, the only newspaper then published here and he printed it.[34] Somebody sent the priest a copy and my arrest was the result. They would have made it warm for me had it not been for the governor.

This is horrible stuff to write but I personally knew of another case where a priest lived openly with three daughters and had children by all of them. All the world knew it. These men had taken holy orders after their wives died. There was a rich man in Chihuahua living openly with his sister. He applied to the legislature for permission to marry her but owing to the presence of so many foreigners in the country it was refused. There was a wealthy man in Mexico City who married his sister. He got a dispensation from the Pope and paid $40,000 for it. Don't you show this to any newspaper man; it might get me in jail again.

While on this point, Wingo and I were invited to dine with the governor once in Chihuahua. When there are guests in Mexico, in a

Mexican family, the women do not sit at the table with the men, but wait and eat alone. They are getting out of this foolish custom now. Well, there were no two plates alike, no two knives and no two forks. They served something like whipped cream and it was put on the table in a cigar box. Before the railroads and Americans got into the country, even the rich had few comforts as we understand the word. They generally ate with their fingers and tortillas. With a piece of tortilla they will scoop up beans and chopped meat, etc. Meat is usually served cut in small pieces to facilitate this. If the meat be in large pieces, they break it with the fingers. Once we had a graduate of their military academy to dinner at Ocampo. Somebody passed him the dish containing English peas. He took it and ate out of it with his knife. No one said anything but no one else ate any peas! They have learned lots since foreigners came into the country.

We finished our maps at Meoqui, took them into Chihuahua and then went on another trip to the western part of the State. We worked all of 1884 and 1885. There was nothing unusual to report. In 1886 I remained in Chihuahua compiling maps for the Banco Minero (Miners' Bank) till the fall, when I was employed by a Chicago company as chief engineer to do survey work for them in Sonora, where I worked for them and a Galveston, Texas, company till 1891. . . .

The Apache Indians of Arizona were on the war path but I managed to keep far enough ahead of them or behind them. I was camped two weeks with my friend Captain Lawton, who was in command of troops pursuing them. Our Major General Leonard Wood was with him as a civilian doctor and I got to know him quite well.[35] Often I have rode up on dead bodies still warm that had been killed and mutilated by the Indians. I had a young American engineer as assistant. He was taken very sick once and I went into a little town by the name of Aconchi and got rooms for him and myself, my men camping in the back yard or corral. We remained there two weeks. The man of the family had to go to Bisbee, Arizona, where he had a contract for packing wood and we travelled together for several days. I was going to Fronteras to continue my work. At Bacuachi I received a courier asking me to send in my monthly statement of expenses. I remained there all next day to make out this statement, write up my mail so as to send it all in by the courier. The Mexican, his wife and four or five children, proceeded and at about 11 o'clock were attacked by Indians and all killed and horribly mutilated. I passed the following day and saw it all. It was horrible and I shuddered to see what I had miraculously escaped.

On this same expedition I hired a white man I found in one of the little towns to take charge of my camp outfit and to move it as I directed. As work advanced it was useless to go back at night to a camp, so I endeavored to have my camp moved up to near where I would stop at night. One morning I gave him explicit directions as to where to put the camp so I could readily find it at night. The country was full of Indians, though no one knew just where they were hiding and I was nervous and careful. I quit work early in the afternoon and went to find my camp. I could find it no where and I and the two or three helpers with me rode all over the country trying to locate it. We failed and then rode into a little town some eight or ten miles away, arriving late in the night, without supper and only a cold and indifferent lunch. I went to a house and woke the people who gave us a place to sleep, putting our animals in the corral. In the morning, bright and early, I was up determined to go out and hunt my camp. As I opened the front door, what should I see but my outfit in a vacant lot across the street, quietly cooking their breakfast, laughing and joking the while. I was mad as a March hare and vented it to the extent of my ability on Mr. Streeter and fired him on the spot. I did not know Streeter when I hired him, but learned afterwards that he was a renegade of the blackest type. He was known as the White Apache, had lived with the Apache Indians many years, knew their ways and spoke their language fluently. It was said he used to visit white ranches and settlements, get information about them for the Indians and lead them in raids on these settlements, killing men, women and children, driving off livestock and destroying or carrying off everything of value. A price was on his head in Arizona, but I did not know it.[36]

I pursued my work and kept my camp close to me all the time, though inconvenient. I finished up, went to Nogales, made my maps and delivered them and went on another trip further south. Nothing of particular interest occurred on this trip except this:

One day about noon we were eating dinner when all of a sudden we heard the galloping of a horse and a man singing and yelling at intervals. Suddenly he rode right up to where we were, seemingly coming out of the ground, reined in his horse and, in bad Spanish, wanted to know who we were. I thought him a Mexican from his bronzed appearance, but he was a white man, an American. I invited him to have dinner with us but he declined although he got down from his horse. I told him who we were and what we were doing. He told us he had a ranch not far from there at a place called Bermudes and invited us to go there. It was on our route . . . and when I finished the work where I was I went over there arriving on February 21, 1888. He had been down to a little town called Muri and was on his way home, drunk and happy and his name was Clark.

At Bermudes I found three brothers, all married to illiterate Mexican or Indian women and with large families of buxom daughters and sons as illiterate as when they were born. The three brothers were fiddlers, they lived in large old fashioned log houses with puncheon floors, the only ones I had seen outside of Georgia. They [farmed], raised hogs, made ham and bacon, tobacco, potatoes, milk, butter, etc. and when I left, they loaded me down with hams, bacon, tobacco and many other good things to eat. They raised the finest Irish potatoes I ever saw and fine onions. This place, El Paso, used to have the finest onions I ever saw. In the early days I have paid as much as 50 cents for one onion but it was as big as a soup plate and sweet so you could eat it like an apple. The seed had been lost and they no longer raise them. It was brought here by the early missionaries. I intended to leave February 22 but they persuaded us to stay over that day. The old men fiddled and the young folks danced all day and all night. They had not seen anybody from the United States for many years. Their history as they told it to me is this: They were from North Carolina, had gone to California in 1849, had accumulated a lot of gold when the civil war broke out and started back to join the confederate army, going by way of Panama. They were shipwrecked on the west coast of Mexico, lost everything they had and were compelled to work for Mexicans for their mere board. They eventually got into the interior, married and finally got where I found them and went to farming on land they did not own, government land. I kept in touch with them for several years, but they are all dead now and their boys and girls are married and as ignorant as ever.

There is a small walled town in eastern Sonora called Bacadehuachic in the heart of the mountains. I rode in there one day about noon and a man came up and spoke in English, although I thought him a Mexican. He was dressed like one and was bronzed to the same color. He said his name was Smith, that he had been a sailor in the confederate navy, had deserted on the west coast of Mexico and gone into the interior. He too had a Mexican woman and was to all intents and purposes a Mexican. He was the school teacher there. The whole town wasn't any bigger than a city square, but it was completely walled in for protection against Indians. It had a beautiful church but no priest. Indeed the church was in bad condition. The walls were covered with oil paintings, doubtless very fine but they too were covered with birdlime. All the churches in Mexico at one time had fine oil paintings, some of them by the best Spanish artists, but everything of that kind has gone to wreck, due to the shiftlessness of the people. Doubtless if these pictures were cleaned, many very fine ones would be found.

I worked for three different companies in Sonora. For the last one I surveyed that neck of Sonora bounded by Arizona on the north, the Colorado River and California on the West, by the Gulf of California on the South and on the East by the rest of Sonora. It is a desert country and I worked from East to West as far as I could go and carry water. Then I took my outfit to Yuma. I and my assistant, a young Canadian engineer just out of McGill College at Montreal, took rooms at the railroad hotel and camped the outfit on the river below Yuma. My plan was to go down the river and enter Mexico again and work East. Yuma is 20 miles from the line and was too far off for a base. I was told there was an American farming near the line, so one day I hired a horse and buggy and drove down there. I found a man by the name of Hill, his wife and a swarm of small children. His house stood astride of the international boundary line and he was farming, rather trying to farm, on both sides. I made arrangements with them for a room for myself and board and to put my camp below on the river. He was to haul my outfit down from Yuma. I sent him to Yuma occasionally to buy supplies and for mail. I kept him and his wagon and team employed. Frequently at meals Mrs. Hill and I and the children were alone. One day she asked to do my washing. I had no washing except underclothing, an occasional woolen shirt and some handkerchiefs and one of my Mexican men usually washed them in camp. I gave her the washing, however. They were poor white trash and he was shiftless and so was she. One day when she and I were alone at the table she asked me if I knew who she was. Of course I had to say that I did not. Then she startled me by saying: "I am a niece of Jefferson Davis. We are from Mississippi, but I belong to a poor branch of the family." Think of that! A niece of Jefferson Davis cooking and washing for a Negro and eating at the same table with him, working for him for wages!

This job finished my work in Sonora and I returned to Nogales to make my maps and reports. This was in 1891, and it was at that time that I was employed by the Nogales people to prepare their land grant case for the Court of Private Land Claims, which eventually got me the appointment of Special Agent of the Department of Justice, in which I served till July, 1901.[37]

After the Nogales case had finally been won, the people gave a banquet and everybody attended except one doctor, who declared he would not eat at the same table with a Negro. Sometime afterwards there was an election for school trustee and this doctor ran against another Democrat. I got out and worked for the other fellow and beat this Negro-hating doctor by a good majority. I have never taken any part in politics and have never voted for a President, chiefly because I have always been in a Territory or in Mexico at presidential elections. . . .

On another occasion at Nogales, there was to be a constitutional convention to frame a constitution, as it was expected Arizona would soon be admitted to statehood. The chairman of the local Republican committee was a Jew by the name of Altschul. Instead of calling a meeting of the committee for it to name candidates and call an election for delegates to the convention, he made up a ticket with his own name at the head, had it printed and issued a call for the election. On the day of the election Jesse Grant, son of General U.S. Grant, another man and myself were in the office of the justice of the peace discussing the situation and decided to defeat Altschul just for the fun of it.[38] We prepared a lot of paper and began to write out tickets. After we had written quite a number—four of us were writing—it occurred to me that that would not do, they would discover our scheme and beat us. So at my suggestion Jesse Grant and I went out to get some of the printed tickets. I went one way and Grant the other. The first man I met was Altschul with a great load of tickets. I asked him for some and he gave me a big bunch of them. I returned to the office and in a few minutes Grant came in with another bunch and we got to work crossing out Altschul's name and writing in the name of our man. The upshot was we beat Altschul by a big majority.[39] He never knew how or who defeated him and he was so chagrined at his defeat he sold his property in Nogales and went to Tegucigalpa in Honduras where he went to raising sugar.

I went into the San Javier Hotel one day in Tucson for dinner. Lieut. R. D. Read of the 10th Cavalry and a classmate of mine was then at a table. As soon as I sat down he got up and went out without his dinner.[40]

Nogales had one newspaper, the *Sunday Herald*, a Republican sheet. The owner and editor was elected to the territorial legislature and left me to run his paper. The legislature could not sit over sixty days. Cleveland was President and was going out and McKinley was coming in. The governor of Arizona was a Democrat appointed by Cleveland. The Republican legislature did not want to meet for fear the governor would appoint Democrats for territorial offices for the next four years and they would have to confirm them. To avoid this, they met, passed a resolution to examine territorial institutions, penitentiary, asylum, etc., and went in a body to inspect them and spent the sixty days in that junket. In the meantime, McKinley appointed a Republican governor; the Legislature met for business and confirmed all the appointees of the Republican governor. During these four months I ran The *Sunday Herald* and had great fun with it.[41]

In one of my trips to El Paso I met Lieut. Ward on the streets. I have already mentioned him several times. He had been dismissed from the Army for drunkenness. He was a dirty, drunken sot when I met him and begged me for a quarter to get something to eat. Although I remembered what he had done about my tent, I gave him the money. I used to meet him on all my trips and if he knew I was in town would hunt me up. In one trip I missed him and on inquiry learned he had been sent to the poor farm where he went crazy, was finally sent home to his people and died.[42]

In 1897, I moved from Nogales [Arizona] to Santa Fe and made my home there till the Court of Private Land Claims ended its labors in 1901. I was in Washington in 1898, 1899, 1900 and 1901. Lieut. Nordstrom was sent to Santa Fe on recruiting duty. I used to see him and his wife, the former Miss [Mollie] Dwyer, almost daily. Neither of them ever spoke to me or noticed me in the slightest degree. He died there [in 1898] leaving his family in poverty and I have never known what become of her and her two daughters.

One dark night I was sitting in the plaza at Santa Fe talking to a Jew merchant when a woman and a small boy passed us. In a few moments the boy came back and asked if one of us was not Lieut. Flipper. I told him I was that man and he said there was a lady who desired to speak to me. I went to see and found a lady in deep mourning sitting on one of the benches. She asked if I knew her and I told her I did not. It was Mrs. [Nicholas] Nolan, my old Captain's widow. [Nolan had died in 1883]. We chatted there for hours recalling old Army experiences. She was in Santa Fe having some work done on the grave of her husband in the National Cemetery there. How different from her sister, Miss Dwyer? She held some position in Washington, a clerkship of some kind, and was doing well, she told me.

While I was Special Agent, Department of Justice, a Mr. Perrin[43] of Riverside, California, and Senator [J. T.] Morgan[44] of Alabama made a desperate fight to save a land grant they claimed in Arizona. Perrin tried to bribe me through a Negro barber at Riverside. The barber wrote me several letters saying he was Mr. Perrin's barber, had heard him speak of me many times, heard him say what a brilliant man I was and so on and so on and that I could easily make a fortune, and that Mr. Perrin would be only too glad to advise me. I turned the letters over to the U. S. Attorney. We answered them but could get no direct evidence against Perrin. Senator Morgan ignored me altogether and when the case went to the Supreme Court at Washington, he had the title papers translated by a translator in the State Department of the government. We were furnished a copy and I was told to examine and criticize it. I wrote a brief and tore it all to pieces. It was [as] poor a translation as I ever saw. The translator had never been in Latin America, knew nothing of the people, their manner of being and of course could not translate correctly. The first word, *alcalde*, he translated chief of police, whereas it means justice of the peace, a judicial not an executive officer. My brief was embodied in a brief by the U. S. Attorney and when Senator Morgan was furnished a copy, he withdrew his translation and adopted mine.

The grant claimants fought me bitterly. The attorneys of the great Cameron family of Pennsylvania, which claimed a big grant in Arizona, filed charges against me alleging that I had done a job of surveying in Sonora for which I had received $1,500, that I had returned to Nogales, got drunk and remained drunk till every penny was gone.[45] These charges were investigated, but every man, woman and child in Nogales knew I never drank liquor of any kind and proved the charges false in every particular. They rallied to my defense.[46]

The same attorneys in another case waited till their case reached the U. S. Supreme Court and in a brief to that Court charged that I had been cashiered from the Army, that I was not therefore eligible to hold any position of honor or trust under the government and that all I had done in the land grant cases was illegal and should be ignored and expunged from the records. The U.S. Attorney answered them and I shall quote what he said. The Supreme Court, in its ruling, ignored the charge absolutely. I was in Washington at the time. As a matter of fact I was not cashiered but dismissed. The difference is that an officer cashiered is barred from any official position of honor or trust under the government. The officer dismissed is not under any such prohibition, but cashiering was abolished in our Army years and years before I ever saw the Army. The U.S. Attorney said:

After the investigation was made, and having before that time had occasion to observe Mr. Flipper very carefully in his work in the Nogales grant (Ainsa vs. U.S., 8688 U.S., 208) at which time he had not been employed by the government, as well as careful inquiry into his private and public character in the community in which he has lived since leaving the Army, I reported to the Attorney General that after careful and full examination I was satisfied that Mr. Flipper was the best equipped, most efficient, competent, reliable and trustworthy man to perform the duties necessary to be performed on behalf of the government in order that its interests might be conscientiously protected in this private land claim litigation in Arizona, and upon that report I was authorized by the Attorney General to continue Mr. Flipper in the service of the government.[47]

Since then he has been constantly under my direction; and observation of his conduct, his work, the efficiency of it as well as the great volume, has only more firmly convinced me, as well as the community in which he has resided since leaving the Army, that he has been more sinned against than sinning.

The excitement and public notoriety occasioned by the private land claim litigation in Arizona has brought upon every one connected with it on behalf of the government the critical, scrutinizing eyes of various adverse interests, as well as the general public, and this is the first attack upon the integrity of the work of any one in the government's service; and every fact upon which this attack is based has been publicly known ever since a time before the inception of this litigation.

My investigation as to Mr. Flipper, and my subsequent observations of him, as well as my associations with the people of Arizona, justify me in stating that no successful attack can be made upon his honesty, his integrity, and his reliability and this is borne out by the general respect and esteem accorded him in the community where he lives and where these land grants are situated.

Having little in common with his race by reason of his talents, attainments, and education; sensitive in the extreme and fully understanding the social lines which the conventionalities of society have drawn against him; compelled by this ostracism to seek his books for companionship and recreation, he has equipped himself both in head and heart so as to attain the respect and confidence of scholars and men of learning who know him or have examined his works. Even the litigants in these cases, with interests adverse to the government, have very largely availed themselves of the work that this man has performed in behalf of the government, and his labors in the office of the United States Attorney for the Court of Private Land Claims for the past five years have been subjected to careful, critical, and rigid scrutiny, and that his duty has been accurately, conscientiously, and faithfully performed has never been questioned till now. Five judges, composing the Court of Private Land Claims, who have observed him carefully and closely since his original appointment, will unite in commending his work and the integrity of it and the man.

In an official and expert capacity, by the side of Special Agent Will M. Tipton, who is recognized all over this country as the most competent Spanish scholar and expert of American birth, Special Agent Flipper, whom it is now sought to discredit, by reason of a court-martial many years ago, and under circumstances never satisfactory to the Army officers who had occasion to know him in the performance of his duties on the frontier, many of whom he served under, has made for himself a name and credit, as a private citizen and a government official, of which any man might well be proud. The record of this court-martial shows that he was convicted of a bare technicality, without culpability attaching thereto. It is within my personal knowledge that he has today the recognized friendship of many officers of the Army who served with him.

As a Special Agent, his work is imprinted in the records of this Court in every Arizona case from the Court below, and he has translated almost every law from the original Spanish which is to be found in the various books and briefs filed in these cases by the government. The accuracy of these translations, even the coloring of a word, has never been questioned by any Spanish scholar of standing, and, as is known to this Court, the improper coloring of a word in translation might lend a meaning very different from that intended; yet all of his translations, investigations, and reports have stood the test of adverse and rigorous investigation.

Had it been sought to attack the credibility of this man in any of the cases on the trials below, it was well known that such an attack could have been successfully and easily overcome by the testimony of citizens of his own community, and I submit that the purpose of this motion should fail of accomplishment here, just as it would have failed in the Court below.

As to the employment of Mr. Flipper by the government, I am responsible for it, and from the time of his appointment and up to the present time I have been and am exceedingly glad that I have had his aid, assistance and support in this trying, difficult, and perplexing litigation. In every Arizona case, save one, the work of this man as a scholar, a translator, a surveyor, an engineer, an expert, a student of Spanish and Mexican law, and as ordinary witness, has been under investigation, and during his whole employment of over [seven] years, after counsel and claimants availing themselves of the results of his labor, criticizing and examining his work, and relying upon it in various instances (vide page 10, Additional Brief of Appellant in this case, filed March 19th, 1898), making no challenge heretofore as to the vast product of his expert skill and ability that is now in cold type before this Court, interspersed throughout the records of the Arizona cases in this Court and the Court below, this is the first time it has ever been questioned.[48]

I was in Washington when these cases were argued. I went often into the Court room but no one there knew who I was. Sometimes I remained in the office of the clerk of the Court in charge of the papers in the cases while the U. S. Attorney was arguing them. In this particular case, one of the Judges expressed a desire to see me and I was called in. I sat by the side of the U. S. Attorney so that I would be known. I served till the Court finished its work and ceased its labors.

When I was in Washington in 1898, I had a bill introduced in Congress to restore me to the Army. I have had a number of bills introduced at different times, but I have never been able to find any one who would take enough interest in the matter to push it. I paid a colored man, Charles Alexander, to make campaign speeches to elect a white man to Congress from Maryland.[49] He was elected and introduced a bill for me, but nothing more was done. I have had no end of disillusionments, many bitter disappointments. Our friend Lyons was Register of the Treasury and he was going to get me back into the Army, no doubt about it, he knew all the Congressmen and had the necessary influence.[50] What did he do? If you will pardon the slang, he "pulled my leg" and nothing more. He would come to me and say: "I have an appointment with Senator—at the Shoreham to-night to discuss your case. He'll order the drinks and cigars and, of course, I'll have to correspond. Let me have a ten or better a twenty. I'll report to-morrow. Run up to the office about eleven." I'd go to his office in the Treasury building only to learn he had failed to see the Senator for this reason or that. He got two or three hundred dollars out of me in this way, and there was never any result whatever. Once he came to me and told me he had arranged for an interview with the President and we were to go to the White House on a certain day and talk the matter all over, with all the time necessary. I was greatly elated over this and was on time the appointed day at Lyons' office. We went to the White House, Lyons expatiating all the way on how well he had arranged the interview, how much influence he had, etc. When we arrived we were shown into the waiting room and I noticed there were fifteen or twenty other persons there, also waiting to see the President. By and by a flunky came in and showed us into another room. We stood in line with our backs to a wall. In a moment a door opened near one end of the line and President McKinley entered. He said: "Good morning, gentlemen. I am glad to see you," shook hands with each and passed out at a door at the other end of the line. The whole thing did not last two minutes and no one spoke a word except the President. The flunky showed us out and that was the end of the interview. Lyons made all sorts of excuses and explanations and promised to arrange another interview, but it never materialized. It dawned on me finally that he had never made an appointment at all. He was just bleeding me.

I received a letter one day from Prof. W. S. Scarborough, in which he expressed his pleasure at knowing I was trying to have my Army record cleared up, said he personally knew the two Senators and all the representatives in Congress from Ohio, had considerable influence with them, as he had obtained various services from them for Wilberforce and he knew he could help me through them.[51] Please send $50 for expenses, etc. I bit, of course, and sent the $50 and $10 and $20, and various sums at various times, but if he ever did anything, I never heard of it. Like Lyons he had found a sucker and bled him to the limit. Alexander mentioned above was true and loyal and spent his own money with some help from me, which I insisted on giving.

There is another man in Washington, an ex-Sergeant of the 9th Cavalry, colored, who came to my hotel one day and introduced himself. I took a liking to him instantly. I hadn't done anything at that time, although I was preparing to move in the matter. He came to urge me to move, and he had the first bill introduced by a Congressman from Wisconsin. He worked like a Trojan, held interviews with Congressmen, took me to call on Congressmen. I remember a long interview he arranged for me with General Joe Wheeler, Congressman from Alabama, and when I got through, Gen. Wheeler said: "That is the damndest outrage I ever heard of and I pledge you my word to make your case a personal case and to push it through the House."[52] Next day McKinley appointed him a Major General in the Army and sent him to Cuba. I never saw him again. He had to resign from Congress to enter the Army and died shortly after returning home from Cuba. My ex-Sergeant friend, whose name is Barney M. McKay, introduced me to a son of Senator Breckenridge of Kentucky, we discussed the case fully and he promised to help through his father who was then absent from Washington sick. He went to Cuba and I never saw him again. McKay has worked all these years for me, is working right now. . . .[53] I have worked hard at all times to have my Army record cleared but I have never had any illusions and have none now. It is uphill work.

At the beginning of the Cuban war I offered my services to the government, but my telegram was never answered. When I was in Washington in 1898, the *Washington Post* published a long article to the effect that the government was considering organizing a volunteer regiment of Negro Cavalry, making me Colonel and Young Lieut-Colonel.[54] I never knew what truth there was in it, it was never done and I made it plain I was not seeking a commission in either the regular or volunteer Army; what I wanted and sought was a clearing up of my Army record, which meant restoral to the regular Army with the grade and rank I would have attained had I not been dismissed. Once restored, the government would have the power to do as it pleased with me.

I have received letters advising me to offer my services now, but shall not do so.[55] At any rate I shall observe the Wilsonian policy of watching and waiting. I am way beyond the age of retirement—fifty-five—and the Army needs young men not sexagenarians. My greatest fear is, however, that this Democratic administration might commission me, if I offered my services now, and send me to Wilberforce or some other school as military instructor. I have a horror of being buried and disposed of in that manner. You know the colleges of the country are entitled to have a military instructor detailed by the War Department. They detail officers in time of peace. Young and Davis served a tour each at Wilberforce and Wilberforce has an application in now, but there is no officer available.[56] Retired officers are detailed when not too old. I would rather die than be so detailed.[57]

In 1881, when my troubles began, I sent a white friend East to raise money for my defense. I had consulted various civilian lawyers and the cheapest of them wanted $1,000 to take the case. This friend went to Washington, interviewed the leading colored men, Pinchback, Terrell, and others whose names I do not now recall, and arranged for a meeting.[58] He met them and made a speech in which he explained all the details of the case. He was asked to leave the hall while they deliberated. After an hour or such a matter he was called in and given a written answer to the effect that if Lieut. Flipper proves his innocence, he can have all the money he needs. Great God! When I wanted the money, not as a gift but as a loan, to *enable* me to prove my innocence. He met with similar rebuffs in New York, Philadelphia, Boston, and other places. Greatly chagrined and depressed, helpless and alone, except that I was surrounded by hyenas, I determined to fight my battle alone and unaided, as I had always done, when, like a bolt out of a clear sky, I received a letter from Captain Merritt Barber of the 16th U.S. Infantry, white, offering to come and defend me. I had never seen or heard of him before, but the Army Register showed me he had been Judge Advocate General at one time in one of the Military Departments and must therefore be a competent military lawyer. I accepted his offer at once, especially as I knew it would cost me nothing, officers not being allowed to charge anything for defending another. I had not had the courage to ask any officer to defend me. He came, lived in my quarters with me and made a brilliant defense, better than any civilian lawyer could have done.[59] But I was doomed beforehand! The prosecuting attorney, called Judge Advocate in military parlance, was the Judge Advocate General of the Department at that time, the man who selected the officers for the court, the man who had to review and did review the proceedings after the trial and of course recommended the approval of his own work. He was Captain John W. Clous of the 24th Infantry, colored.[60] What irony of fate, no?

When I was in Washington in 1898, I received an invitation from Mrs. Mary Church Terrell to dine with her one Sunday.[61] I had never seen her but I had met Judge Terrell several times. I went, of course. There were at the table Judge and Mrs. Terrell, Mrs. Paul Laurence Dunbar and yours truly.[62] The conversation was principally about

Merritt Barber (Fort Davis National Historic Site).

woman suffrage. About 2:45 P.M., Mrs. Terrell excused herself abruptly at the table and said she had to be at church at 3 o'clock. She, Mrs. Dunbar and the Judge rose from the table and I did the same. The ladies left, the Judge lingering. I had not been invited to go to church with them and nothing was said in any way to relieve me of what was an embarrassing situation. The Judge hesitated and it seemed plain that he wanted me to go, so I said something and withdrew. I was impressed with the ordinariness of the dinner, especially the lettuce salad that was all wilted and appeared to have been prepared two or three hours before it was served or was a left over. I worried quite a bit over the incident and reached the conclusion that they had invited me merely to see what Lieut. Flipper looked like and to size him up, and that the result had been unsatisfactory to them. She spoke in the towns of East Texas two or three years ago and was invited to come here, but did not come. I never knew why.

In July, 1901, having completed my labors with the Court of Private Land Claims as Special Agent, I received a telegram from New York from the Manager of the Balvanera Mining Company asking me to meet him in El Paso on a date he named, prepared to go to Mexico with him as resident engineer of the company. I met him but did not go down till the following August. This company was a New York company and William G. McAdoo, the present Secretary of the U. S. Treasury, was President of the company.[63] Two factions soon developed in the company over the choice of the General Manager and it got to the point where each faction refused to furnish any money unless its own man was manager. Fortunately we took out enough money from the mines to pay the employees. I was left in charge of the property while the manager went to New York to try to bring about some sort of an agreement. As soon as he reached New York the other faction sent a man down to oust me and take charge of the property. He came down, came to the property and I gave him a room to sleep in. Next morning, when he got up, he told me who he was and ordered me off the premises and out. I didn't waste any words with him but told him I had possession and if he got obstreperous I would put *him* off. I had two men besides myself. Well, after arguing a while, he went up town to get his breakfast and when he came back, he found his baggage in the street and one of my men watching it till his return. He never got on the premises again. He then went into the courts, but I didn't fear that. I learned one day that he had bribed the judge to put me out by force. Whether true or not I never knew, but I went at once to the judge and told him what I had heard and it so scared him that he did nothing. The matter hung along for five or six months till the fellow got tired and left. I never had any more trouble.

In 1905, the Balvanera Mining Company, unable to agree on anything else, decided to sell the property to Col. William C. Greene, the Cananea Copper King. As soon as the sale was consummated, I received a telegram from the Vice-President, A.B. Fall, now U. S. Senator from New Mexico, asking if I would accept a position on the staff of the company in the legal department, to which I answered in the affirmative.[64]

We did nothing in the way of mining for about a year, but during that time Col. Greene brought, or sent out in charge of some mining engineer, parties of rich capitalists to look over the mines with the view of interesting them and having them buy stock in the company. He ordered me to prepare a kitchen and dining room to take care of these people. I got a Chinese cook and helper, fixed up a kitchen and dining room, bought chickens, sent men to scour the country for eggs, had provisions, including wines, brought out from Chihuahua, etc. Col. Greene came with the first party of millionaires from New York and Boston. At the first meal he ordered me to sit at the head of the table. We served excellent meals, the best ever served in those mountains. We had oranges, limes, and aguacates (alligator pears) grown right there in the town. For a whole year, almost every two or three weeks, sometimes oftener, there was a party of capitalists there. I had orders to feed any foreigners, particularly Americans, passing through and there were quite a number at one time and another. Flipper's restaurant became famous all over Chihuahua.

One of his engineers stayed there a month or two, Gen. Henry Ide Willey. He had been Surveyor General of California and hence the title. Gen. Willey didn't like the Chinaman's coffee, so one day he went up town to buy a coffee pot. He found a Russian coffee pot and bought it. . . . That day at dinner there were only three of us, I at the head of the table, Gen. Willey on my left and the wife of another engineer on my right. Gen. Willey opened his new pot, had the Chinaman bring him some freshly ground coffee and boiling water. He put in the coffee and then the water, closed the pot and turned it over, according to directions. It came unfastened and spilled the hot water all over him. He swore like a trooper. Then he had more coffee and water brought and did it all over, with care to see the pot was properly closed. Then he turned to the lady and with a courtly bow, said: "Will the little lady kindly excuse my French?" It was so ludicrous I could hardly keep from laughing.

Gen. Willey brought his wife out from California on another occasion. He was over fifty and she could not have been over twenty-five or thirty at the outside and a most beautiful woman. I saw something one day I know she would have given the world to keep covered up and hidden from the vulgar gaze of mere man. I do not remember what accident showed it to me, but I saw it, saw it all and plainly as could be. She had a snake tattooed all around her right arm just below the shoulder. The snake went around twice with the head pointing toward the shoulder and the tail toward the hand. It was tattooed in natural colors and on her pure white skin showed up brilliantly, gorgeously and beautifully. The General tried to apologize after she had gone by explaining how she came to have it, but I knew both of them would have preferred not to have had me see it.

Finally work was begun in the mines with a big crew of Mexicans and Americans and I was kept pretty busy. The company had mines in Sonora and in Chihuahua and it was my business to keep them all out of trouble with the authorities and I was in the saddle pretty nearly all the time. There were lots of interesting incidents, perhaps the most interesting was this one:

Twelve miles from Ocampo the company had a promising mine and it developed into a rich property. It was on the land of another American mining company and our company tried to buy the surface ground over its own claims, but the other company refused to sell;

they didn't want us there and put all sorts of obstacles in the way. Col. Greene went to the home office of the company in Cleveland, Ohio, but they would not listen to him. Then he wired me to have the courts condemn the land. We had built shacks for our men. [The other company] tried to tear them down and several fights resulted. They arrested our men when building a telephone line.

We had a store with groceries and clothing for the men. They tried to close that. Our store keeper, an American, would telephone me when they ordered him to close and I would rush over. I gave him orders not to close the store under any circumstances. Col. Greene sent a lawyer from Tombstone, Arizona, to help me. He was a Virginian, had learned to speak Spanish in Arizona but knew no Mexican law. I sent him to this mine with orders not to close the store under any circumstances, if the court ordered him to close, not to do so, but to let the court send its own officers and close it. I knew they would not do that. Well, he went over and next morning I got a telephone message from him saying he had an interview with the superintendent of the other company and had consented to close the store. If you never saw a mad man, you ought to have seen me. I jumped on my mule, rushed over there and opened that store and it stayed open. I am as stubborn as a mule and never so happy as when someone has the temerity to oppose me. Be warned. I fired that lawyer on the spot and told him to get out and report to Col. Greene, and he left. I had already brought suit to condemn the land and won it. The other company appealed to the Federal District Court and I appealed by wire to the Supreme Court in Mexico City and got a decision. The local court then ordered the company to make us a deed to the land and us to pay them $800 silver, the appraised value of the land. I walked all around and over Ocampo one whole day with a *mozo* (servant) carrying a sack of 800 Mexican silver dollars, trying to find the lawyer of the other company to make a tender of the money, but he hid from me. At the end of office hours I reported to the court and was ordered to deposit the money with the County Treasurer, which I did, and the next day the court itself signed the deed and the company still has it and the land. This stopped all trouble.

Col. Greene sent another lawyer out to help me. He was a young man from Kansas City and his wife was from Rochester, New York. They didn't know a word of Spanish, although they were nice people. I wanted him to go over to the Trinidad mine in Sonora. They were having trouble over there about taxes; the authorities were trying to collect taxes not due, trying to rob us in fact. My new lawyer showed no disposition to go and I suspected he did not want to leave his wife in Ocampo. I suggested that he take her along. It was a five or six days' ride westward over the mountains for them and I had ridden it in four days. I also suggested going to El Paso, through New Mexico and Arizona and down to Hermosillo, the capital of Sonora, all by rail. At Hermosillo he could hire a carriage and ride right to the door of the superintendent's office in Trinidad. He didn't go. Col. Greene came out and fired him. I never had any help worth the name.

All over Mexico I have been treated by Americans and other foreigners on an absolute equality, except in one instance. I have been invited to dinners, balls, entertainments of all kinds, etc. My first experience of this kind was in Mexico City in 1887. I went down with the Manager of the Sonora Land Company, his wife and Father Gallagher, all of Chicago. Father Gallagher stopped at the Iturbide Hotel and we at the Jardin. Mr. Kruse received a telegram that his brother had shot himself—it turned out that a revolver had accidentally gone off and the ball entered his foot, nothing serious—and he and Mrs. Kruse hurried back to Chicago. One day I went in to dinner and sat down alone at our usual table. At another table there were two gentlemen and three ladies, all Americans. As soon as I sat down, one of the men came over and asked if I spoke English—he had heard me speaking Spanish. Then he wanted to know if I wasn't a colored man and I told him I was. He then invited me to go over and eat at their table, which I did. They told me they were from Memphis, Tennessee, and were just travelling for pleasure. I went around the city with them and had a really nice time till they left. We ate together in the hotel and at other places till they left.

The *Globe-Democrat* sent a man down to Mexico City to write it up and he and I planned to see the whole city by night. We took a section every night and kept it up till we had been in every street and every nook and hole in the city. We got into some pretty tough places at times and got lost a number of times. The police in Mexico are never seen on the street at night. Each one had a lantern, pistol, rifle, and a club in those days. They would leave the lantern in the middle of a crossing and if one was needed, all you had to do was to pick up the lantern and he would come out of his hiding place in a hurry. Whenever we got lost all we had to do was to go to a lantern and raise it and ask the policeman to tell us how to get out and get home. We also planned to eat, take at least one meal, in every eating place in the city: hotel, restaurant and what not and we did, but, as this was done in the day time, we had no trouble, but we ate trash we wouldn't have touched under other circumstances.

When Mr. Kruse came back he gave a dinner for the Minister of Public Works. The latter did not attend but sent a representative. At the table were this representative, Mr. Kruse, myself, Gen. [H.N.] Frisbie and a half dozen Mexicans. We had a swell dining room on the third floor of Omarini's, the Delmonico of Mexico. I saw something there I never saw before or since. We had a long dinner in courses and a different wine with each course. When the claret was served, three or four buckets of hot water were brought in and set around the table on the floor. The bottles of claret were placed in these buckets till the wine was warm. It was then served. Gen. Frisbie was the representative of the Pacific Mail Steamship Company in Mexico. He had a daughter married to a Portuguese Count, the most worthless man I ever knew. He took a great fancy to me and I have got him out of the gutter a number of times and taken him home. Gen. Frisbie arranged to have me made a Professor in the Military Academy of Mexico at Chapultepec, but I declined because it was necessary to become a Mexican citizen in order to get it.[65]

I want to add this. Father Gallagher and I visited many of the thousand and one churches in the City of Mexico and were entertained by the priests at many of them. One day we visited the Archbishop and found him at the cathedral just at the close of a service. He could speak no English and Father Gallagher no Spanish, so they conversed in Latin. This was the only time in my life I ever heard two persons converse in Latin. I could catch a word here and there but not enough to understand what they were talking about.

In Chihuahua for years I ate at the Delmonico Restaurant, a really first class place run by two Italians. I frequently went in with other Americans or was invited to eat at their tables. I remember particularly Mister and Mrs. Norval Welsh of San Antonio, Texas. If they were in there I had to eat at their table or if they caught me when they were going to a meal, I had to go with them. Mrs. Welsh was a Maverick, the wealthiest family in Texas and she was quaintly southern. She had travelled all over Europe, all over the world. She took special delight in saying "'taters" for sweet potatoes, "tote" and such southern words. I had the pleasure of entertaining them at Ocampo. They always travelled with a colored maid and how she wondered to see me eating at the same table with them.

I was told that a white man once protested to the owner of the Delmonico restaurant about my eating there. I had just paid for my dinner and gone out. The proprietor took my money out of the drawer, looked it over and over, then looked at the money of that man and answered him: "I see no difference between your money and his. Besides, that man is a gentleman. He comes in here alone sometimes, sometimes with the best people in town, he is often invited to leave his table and go to theirs and you are the only man who has kicked. Nothing doing."

There is an old Swede in Chihuahua. He sold a mine in our camp for $60,000 American money. He went to Chihuahua City and in four or five months he didn't have a penny. He was about 70 years old at that. He actually got down to begging for something to eat. Whenever I was in Chihuahua, if I saw him about meal time, I would invite him to go and eat with me and I used to think he waylaid me at times to get the invitation. I was told that he was in the restaurant one day eating at the invitation of some one else, when a man stepped up to him and began to berate him because he ate with a nigger. They say the old man laid his knife and fork down, wiped his mouth with his napkin, folded that and laid it down, and got up and cursed that man for everything he could think of, till the fellow slunk out of the place without eating his own dinner. The old man sat down and finished his meal and they say the room was full of blue streaks for more than an hour.

I always stopped at the Robinson House in Chihuahua and had done so for years. This hotel was first opened and always kept by an American family. At this particular time it was kept by a Mr. and Mrs. Hood. I went in one day about noon to wash for dinner in 1910. As I stepped into the court Mrs. Hood came up, took me by the lapels of my coat with both hands and said to me: "Lieut. Flipper, I notice you don't eat here. Why don't you? You are paying for it." I told her I had eaten so long at the Delmonico that, when meal time came, I felt an irresistible force impelling me in that direction. She insisted on my eating there and I went in to dinner. The meals were good and the service too, but the meals were *table d'hote*, that is, you had to eat what was set before you, there was no choice. The Delmonico had a long bill of fare from which to choose and the service was first class in every respect. Every day in the year they had roast beef, roast mutton, roast veal, roast pork and roast chicken and short orders without limit, game, fish, oysters, etc. Usually for dinner I had a bowl of soup, a roast, two or three vegetables, a salad, a dessert, coffee and cream that were coffee and cream, butter and bread and a plenty of everything. My dinner cost me usually 90¢ or 45¢ our money. Every day there were three or four special dishes for the day, for instance, Irish stew, macaroni or spaghetti, Italian style, and codfish Biscayan style (*Bacalao a la Vizcaina*), this latter a delicious dish. I am specially fond of soups, salads and stews.

There is a Foreign Club in Chihuahua. Whenever I went to the city, the first member I met would greet me with: "Have you a card to the Club?" If I had not, he'd go and get me one, which would give me the privileges of the Club for two weeks, longer than I usually remained in town. I enjoyed this courtesy for five or six years. In 1910, I went to Chihuahua and in the early morning after my arrival, I went to the American Stationery and Photo Supply Company to get an American newspaper. Before giving me the paper, Mr. Pigott, one of the proprietors, asked me if I had a card to the Club and I told him no, I had just got in the night before late. He went to get me one. He came back after a while and told me that a rule had been made not to issue any more cards to me. He raged and swore and said it was a damn outrage, etc. He promised to let me know who had been the instigator of this rule and on my next visit to Chihuahua told me it had been done by a new member, a Canadian by the name of Gillies. Gillies lived in Georgia at one time and married a woman in Rome, Georgia. He and his family live here now, refugees like myself. The Club got in a wrangle over the admission of Mexicans and dwindled and is now practically closed.

I've had my experiences, both grave and gay. Some of them have slipped out of my memory or do not recur to me as I write. Some have little importance and so I will stop here. I may tell you more from time to time.

2

ARMY AND CIVILIAN LETTERS

[Henry Flipper's gift for accurate observation and description of his environment was already well developed by 1878, only a year after his West Point graduation. In that year, he published his detailed memoir, *The Colored Cadet at West Point*.

Arriving at his first western duty station in January, 1878, the young second lieutenant sent a letter to the historian of his West Point Class of 1877. It was a brief but valuable description of frontier Fort Sill, Oklahoma, only nine years after its 1869 founding by General Philip H. Sheridan during his 1868-1869 Indian War campaign.

The Fort Sill of today remains one of the Army's major installations, familiar to many veterans as the long-time home of the Field Artillery Center.]

Fort Sill, Indian Territory, January 4, 1878.

I received orders to join my company [Troop A of the Tenth Cavalry, a regiment of black troops with white officers] on the 6th of December, 1877. At Houston, Texas, I met Lieutenant Colonel [John W. "Black Jack"] Davidson of my regiment, who informed me that my company was under marching orders for Fort Sill, Indian Territory. I was instructed from San Antonio to proceed to Fort Sill and there await my company. I went from Houston to Caddo, Indian Territory, by rail. At Caddo, I took the stage. After a very disagreeable journey of one hundred and sixty miles, I reached Fort Sill Tuesday evening, January 1st.

The quarters here are double, that is, each house contains two sets of quarters. Each set has a front room, a bedroom, dining-room, kitchen, and two bedrooms in the attic for servants. The government has furnished me with quite an amount of furniture, tables, chairs, stoves, bedstead, etc. The officers live singly or two or three together, there being no single mess for all as at West Point.

The post is garrisoned both by cavalry and infantry. It is a twelve-company post, beautifully situated on or near Medicine Bluffs, near the junction of Medicine and Cache creeks. The quarters are all stone and well plastered. They are built on the sides of a square, the space inclosed being the general parade. Altogether the post is a good one and a pleasant one at which to be stationed.[1]

[A few months later we have further evidence that the precise perception characteristic of Flipper's personality was present early in his career. On August 28, 1878, while serving as Officer of the Day at Fort Sill, he submitted the following report.]

The Officer of the Day suggests that the word 'Daylight' [to sound reveille] is too indefinite. The interval from 'Daylight' to sunrise is 30 minutes more or less. At this season the sun rises 1 to 2 minutes later each day... [T]he time of 'Daylight' has grown later and later each day until now 'Daylight' and reveille are nearly coinciding. The Officer of the Day suggests that some determinate time be fixed upon for reveille, as 'Daylight' changes from day to day and is therefore vague.[2]

[Several months later, Flipper reported for duty at Fort Elliott, Texas, on March 6, 1879. Every newly commissioned West Point graduate, including those assigned to the cavalry, had followed a civil engineering curriculum. This background proved indispensable when establishing and maintaining Army posts on the frontier. Fort Elliott, located in the isolated Texas Panhandle near present-day Mobeetie, was founded in 1874, just five years prior to Flipper's arrival. The young black cavalryman's technological education was put to immediate practical use, as he describes in a March 29, 1879, letter from Fort Elliot.]

....After getting here on the 6th instant and being fixed up in a manner measurably comfortable, I was made, or rather detailed, as a sort of post engineering officer and ordered to survey the reservation and post, make maps showing plan of post, plan of all buildings, their elevations, mark the corners of the reservation, set up a sun-dial and to make drawings and estimates for cavalry stables....[3]

[In the same 1879 letter from Fort Elliot, Flipper commented further on his fifteen months of frontier duty and expressed satisfaction with his miliary career. He also related information about the composition of his precocious autobiography, *The Colored Cadet at West Point.* Furthermore, he analyzed (or possibly rationalized) the psychological consequences of the social ostracism he had endured as a cadet at West Point from 1873 to 1877. He concluded by reporting a marked improvement in relationships with his former classmates after they had embarked on active duty and were free of the peer pressure that prevailed at the Military Academy.]

Fort Elliot, Texas, March 29, 1879.

MY DEAR SIR: At this, my very first opportunity, I want to write and thank you for your kind words conveyed to me in your letter of the 3rd ultimo. I was in the field, scouting, when I received it, and was not then in condition to write you a reply. Returning to [Fort] Sill on the 20th ultimo, I found orders for my company to proceed at once to this post and take station. This, of course, further delayed my writing to you.... It is certainly gratifying to me to have my book [*The Colored Cadet at West Point*] so well spoken of.... You can easily imagine how I felt upon receiving your letter, when I assure you I had not yet seen the printed book and knew nothing of how it was being received by the public. It was after much hesitancy that I consented to publish it and I con-

West Point cadet Henry O. Flipper (The United States Military Academy Archives).

fess I was not without doubts as to the propriety of doing so. The manuscript (original part) was all written before I graduated, but here and there on fly leaves of books, in blank books, on bits of paper kept in a box and in some cases, on the margins of book leaves. After graduating (October [June 11], '77), I compiled the manuscript and put in the newspaper articles. I could have published a full year before I did so.

I certainly feel now that my isolation was in no wise to be regretted. I have tried to state somewhere in the book that I was far from being unhappy and content, except at moments which may have come to me under a contrary state of affairs. It was partly to remove the impression that my course at West Point was a sort of martyrdom that I consented to publish my own views on the matter. How easy it would have been for the cadets to have caused my failure! Had they recognized me fully there is no doubt that I could have been unconsciously led to neglect my studies and duties and have made my success so doubtful, as, with the weight of opinion and feelings against me, to have caused my complete failure. But that was not the case, and I was driven to seek in my books, for which I have a strong, natural fondness, that pleasure denied me in the non-association of cadets with me. Circumstances, which were under their control, but providentially left neglected, have made me what I am. The view the public seems to have taken of the matter both amused and pained me— amused me because it was a blunder, into which they had gone blindfold, and pained me because it cast a shadow of undeserved reproof on some who did not at all merit it. These were additional reasons for the publication. I wanted to remove that stain, and the more so because many of those same cadets, removed from the influences that hedge West Point, have since treated me not simply as a brother officer, but as a classmate, and have asked my cooperation in measures adopted and undertaken by the class. We keep up all our class organizations, and although I was not—or, if ever, seldom—invited to share their responsibilities and benefits at the Academy, I am now welcomed by direct and special invitation into them all. But I must not tire you with what is of but little interest to you. For the article in the *Progress* sent me by you, please accept my many sincere thanks. Assuring you that my after life— my mode of conduct for the future—shall be modeled on my life at the Academy, and that I shall never, Deo volente, swerve from that Christian sense of duty that ever leads to success in all things where God is our assistant, I beg to be, yours very sincerely.

HENRY O. FLIPPER,
Second Lieutenant Tenth Cavalry.[4]

[Two years and four months later, Flipper's optimism had turned to alarm and then to despair. He was convicted in a court-martial trial during the fall of 1881 at Fort Davis, Texas, and dismissed from the Army on June 30, 1882.

Flipper's earliest account of what befell him at Fort Davis in 1881 was his statement in his own defense read by him to the Court on December 6, 1881, the twenty-eighth day of the trial. On the advice of his counsel, Captain Merritt Barber, who had been a civilian attorney before entering the Army during the Civil War, Flipper chose not to testify on the witness stand. Instead, he read aloud to the Court the following written statement.]

Gentlemen of the Court:

To the first charge and its specification in this case I declare to you in the most solemn and impressive manner possible that I am perfectly innocent in every manner, shape or form; that I have never myself nor by another appropriated, converted or applied to my own use a single dollar or a single penny of the money of the Government or permitted it to be done, or authorized any meddling with it whatever. Of *crime* I am *not* guilty. The funds for which I was responsible I kept in my own quarters in my trunk, the trunk I procured at West Point and have used ever since I entered the service. My reasons for keeping them there were that as I was responsible for their safety I felt more secure to have them in my own personal custody. From May 28th to July 8th the weekly verification of funds ceased, but I regularly put the weekly accumulations into the trunk and never took a dollar out except to pay the beef bill for June which was paid in checks at the request of Mr. Henning whose contract had expired and who gave as his reason for wishing checks that he intended to leave this section of country. This was previous to the verification of July 8th, from which date up to August 9th the funds of the last fiscal year were never touched by me. August 9th was the first verification covering the July bills of officers who were in the field. The commanding officer declined to verify the statements until the money was presented and I took out about $250 I think, enough with what the Commissary Sergeant [Carl Ross] advanced to satisfy the statement. The money so transferred to the present fiscal year to cover those bills due was principally silver and after verification the entire amount just as it was verified was put into my trunk in a cigar box and the next evening when I transferred to Lieut. [Frank H.] Edmunds was turned out of the box on to the desk.[5] That morning, August 10th, I had taken the checks pertaining to last fiscal year to the Commissary Sergeant to make a letter of transmittal and when I took them out as well as when I returned them to the envelope after the letter was written, there was a large amount of currency in that envelope, apparently enough to satisfy what ought to be there although I did not count it as it appeared to be all correct.

My servant [Lucy Smith] having no place to keep her clothes safely had asked me if she could put some of it in that trunk and I granted her permission; keeping the keys myself, and only handing them to her when she desired to get something out or put something in, and then but for a short time; cautioning her to be very careful of my goods and papers and to never leave anything unlocked or insecure. I had no reason to question the honesty of any of the persons about my house as I never missed anything that attracted my attention, and when the officers searched that trunk and failed to find the funds which I had put in there three days before I was perfectly astounded, and could hardly believe the evidence of my own senses. As to where that money went and who took it I am totally ignorant.

To the second charge and its specifications I make this statement: On the 2nd day of May last I received a dispatch from Col. [Michael P.] Small directing me not to transmit any more funds.[6] I knew he was absent and as it was the first time during my charge of the Commissary Department of the post that the Chief Commissary had been absent I construed it to mean that every thing pertaining to funds was suspended till his return, but I continued to submit the actual cash I had on hand through May when it was discontinued as it seemed to me unnecessary to submit funds and not forward the statements. Sometime in May the actual cash on hand did not meet the amount for which I was responsible. I was owing a considerable bill myself which it was not convenient to pay, and as there was a large amount due me from men and laundresses I believed that my shortage was accounted for in that way, but as the funds were not to be transmitted for some time it did not occasion me any uneasiness, as I felt confident of getting it in by the time it would be required. From the last of May the funds were not verified until the 8th of July, when I was called upon by the commanding officer to submit them at once. Upon counting my funds I found I was $1440 short, but of that my own accounts were due since April amounting to above five hundred dollars and I had not collected anything outstanding or given any attention to the matter. After verification the commanding officer directed me to transmit the funds as soon as possible and I directed the Commissary Sergeant to make the invoices and receipts. I had trouble in getting checks, but I knew Company "A" 10th Cavalry, my own company, was coming into the post on Sunday the 10th of July, as it did; and as it had two months' pay in checks I thought I could get enough from them and procure enough from dues to make up what I was lacking and I made the entry on the weekly statements that the funds had been sent feeling confident that I could get them and send them in a day or two. But in this I was disappointed as the post trader cashed the checks the day after the arrival of the company. I then learned the Chief Commissary had left San Antonio again and I communicated with Homer Lee & Co., from whom I expected a considerable sum of money on account of my book, to remit to my credit to the San Antonio National Bank as they had informed me they would do as soon as they got in statements from their agents. They did not do so and I continued the entry on the weekly statements and retained them expecting to get every day notice of funds deposited. The $74 from Homer Lee & Co., was deposited after my arrest and is all I have ever received from them. On the morning of the 10th of August I took what checks I had to the Commissary Sergeant and directed him to make a letter of transmittal of them and searched for checks to meet the money I had, expecting daily a deposit from Homer Lee & Co., but there were no checks to be procured and no deposit was made. On the 13th of August when I left my house with Mr. [W.S.] Chamberlain[7] I have every reason to believe and do believe that all the funds for which I was responsible was in the trunk and in my quarters except the $1440 check which I have already explained, and the amount of my Commissary bill for July which I had not paid. As to their disappearance I have no privity or knowledge and am not responsible except to make the amount good, and that I have done.

As to my motives in the matter alleged in the first specification of the second charge [a false statement to Shafter] I can only say that some time before I had been cautioned that the commanding officer would improve any opportunity to get me into trouble, and although I did not give much credit to it at the time, it occurred to me very prominently when I found myself in difficulty; and as he had long been known to me by reputation and observation as a severe, stern man, having committed my first mistake I indulged what proved to be a false hope that I would be able to work out my responsibility alone, and avoid giving him any knowledge of my embarrassment.

Henry O. Flipper
2d Lieut., 10th Cavalry[8]

[It is undeniable that Flipper had been seriously negligent in his official stewardship of government funds. The reasons for such uncharacteristic behavior are still unclear today. When the prosecution was unable to present evidence or testimony proving embezzlement, Flipper was duly found innocent of that charge. In the matters of the false statements and the bad check, however, the tribunal obviously found his explanation of these in his statement to the Court to be unconvincing.

Despite the emotional trauma and public disgrace accompanying his dismissal, Flipper remained proud of his positive achievements as the Regular Army's first and, in his day, only black commissioned officer. As a civilian, sixteen months after his dismissal, Flipper wrote to a newspaper correspondent in reply to the latter's publication of a recent interview with him. Using the third person, Flipper in El Paso, Texas, sent a letter to F. W. May on November 15, 1883, which included a typically detailed account of some of his active duty accomplishments.]

....He has occupied all positions that usually fall to the lot of the young officer, and some that many officers never occupy. He has been post adjutant, quartermaster, commissary, signal officer, battalion adjutant, post engineering officer, has even been commanding officer of Fort Sill, Indian Territory, and has commanded two troops of cavalry. He has repeatedly been selected for important professional duty. In 1879 he built the telegraph line from Fort Elliott, Texas, 52 miles toward Fort Supply, I. T. He also surveyed and mapped the military reservation at the former post, an area of 25 square miles. He also set up at the place a sundial, constructed under his direction. At Fort Sill he succeeded in draining 40 miles of marshes. He prides himself on this feat, because two other officers had failed to do the same thing. One of the officers was a graduate of Heidelberg and an engineer. [Flipper] also surveyed and opened a road from Fort Sill to Gainesville, Texas.[9]

[By February, 1884, Flipper had secured a position with an American company surveying land in northern Mexico and began his second career as the first black American civil engineer. He was enthusiastic about his new surroundings, and romanticized the Mexican people as simple and happy "Arcadians." His admiration for them was tempered mainly by a Puritanical morality derived from his strict parents and pre-West Point education in Reconstruction Georgia at New England-sponsored American Missionary Society schools. On February 9, 1884, the El Paso *Lone Star* quoted a letter on its front page from Flipper in Mexico.]

I like this sort of life and may yet adopt it, or something like it, for my mode of passing all my days. I detest public life, or publicity of any kind. The simple life of these Arcadians interests me. Their simple habits, their few and easily supplied wants make them the happiest people on earth, were their women virtuous. It seems that women do not lose their caste here when they lose their virtue, nor the men either who rob them of it.[10]

[Over the years Flipper retained a sincere sense of national loyalty and a conservative patriotism that were never dimmed by the deep hurt he had to live with after the disintegration of his military dream.

At the outbreak of the Cuban crisis with Spain, in February of 1898, he was in El Paso, Texas, serving as a Justice Department Special Agent for the U.S. Court of Private Land Claims. Although almost forty-two years old, he sent the following telegram to Secretary of War Russell A. Alger volunteering for national service.[11] The telegram was never answered.]

El Paso, Texas
February 24, 1898.

To the Secretary of War
Washington, D.C.

As graduate U.S. Military Academy, Class Seventy-seven, my services are at disposal of War Department in any capacity in which they can be utilized in event of war.

HENRY OSSIAN FLIPPER
Now Special Agent, Department of Justice.[12]

TWO BLACK FRONTIERSMEN
Henry Flipper and Estevanico

[Despite the psychological trauma and frustration of his Army career, Henry Flipper continued to exercise his rich intellectual capacities. He accomplished this while leading a rugged and hazardous engineering career on the southwestern and Mexican frontier from 1883 to 1919. He developed a scholarly interest in the history of the region. This was facilitated by his mastery of the Spanish language that enabled him to pursue research in original sources whenever he could obtain them. In addition, he studied important secondary authorities and, as early as 1896, was familiar with the work of such pioneer scholars as Adolphe Bandelier.

By 1896, Flipper had turned his attention to the little-known role of black people in the Spanish colonization of North America. As he expressed it in his publication reprinted below, "It is my purpose to publish at some future day as complete an account as possible of the part taken by Negroes in the discovery, conquest and civilization of the Southwest country. To this end I am collecting documents of all kinds."

Naturally, he was attracted to the sixteenth century southwestern exploits of the African adventurer known as Estevanico (c. 1500-May, 1539). Just as the black Estevanico had challenged geographical frontiers, Flipper himself had challenged racial frontiers.

The result of his research was a booklet published in late 1896, at Nogales, Arizona Territory, bearing the intriguing title, *Did a Negro Discover Arizona and New Mexico?* In it, Flipper became the first scholar to advance the claim that Estevanico, a black African, was the first foreigner to enter the lands that later became New Mexico and Arizona while serving as advance guide for the Spanish exploring expedition of Marcos de Niza in 1539. When writing on this topic, Flipper had the advantage of personal field experience in much of the territory involved. Flipper's work was read by Dr. W. E. B. Du Bois, America's preeminent African American historian, who incorporated Flipper's conclusion in his own account of Estevanico's historical significance.[1]

The fruits of Flipper's research also provided him an opportunity to express racial pride beyond his recognition of Estevanico's accomplishments. Such opportunities were rare in the racially tense America of the 1890s. They enabled him to conclude his study with the hitherto unpublished fact that "there were Negroes in Florida, Texas, Arizona, New Mexico and Kansas nearly a century before the Anglo Saxon set foot upon the North American continent, for Drake was not born till 1540." This is particularly interesting because most historians still date the first arrival of black Africans in North America in 1619, just one year prior to the *Mayflower* landing at Plymouth.

In his analysis, Flipper was also the first scholarly investigator to clarify that Stephen (Estevanico) and Dorantes were two separate persons. Stephen was a slave and Dorantes was his master. Some modern historians still remain confused on this important point and continue to refer to Estevanico as "Stephen Dorantes."

Furthermore, while chronicling his research discoveries, Flipper contributed the first published English translation of extensive portions of Pedro de Castañeda's eyewitness account of Francisco de Coronado's exploration of the Southwest from 1540 to 1542.

Flipper sought to rehabilitate Estevanico's personal reputation, which had been severely damaged by Castañeda's narrative. Flipper maintained that Castañeda uncritically accepted American Indian allegations that Estevanico had exploited them by excessive greed and lechery and that the Indians were merely trying to justify their slaying of the black man.

The extremely rare document reprinted below is a newly edited copy of Flipper's 1896 publication. The editor discovered the original

Flipper in the 1890s—the picture was taken at Tucson, Arizona Territory (Arizona Historical Society, Tucson).

in the Fisk University Library, Nashville, Tennessee. It is published here by courtesy of Fisk University.

Flipper chose to use the English version, Stephen, of Estevanico's name.]

DID A NEGRO DISCOVER ARIZONA AND NEW MEXICO?
By Henry O. Flipper

"A Negro Discovered New Mexico," is the caption of an article in the A[frican] M[ethodist] E[piscopal] Review for July, 1896,[2] by Professor Richard R. Wright [Sr.],[3] an erstwhile classmate of mine at the Atlanta University.[4] The article has just been brought to my attention. As it treats of a matter of the greatest interest to me, I will endeavor to give such details as are in my possession. It is my purpose to publish at some future day as complete an account as possible of the part taken by Negroes in the discovery, conquest and civilization of the Southwest country. To this end I am collecting documents of all kinds. I have seen and have copied mention of Negroes in many documents and books of the period, but details are meagre, incomplete and unsatisfactory. I have a copy, in Spanish, of [Pedro Francisco de] Castañeda's narrative of [Francisco Vasquez de] Coronado's expedition into what are now Arizona, New Mexico and Kansas in 1540 and 1542. The original is not known to exist, but there is, in the Lenox Library in New York City, a copy of the original made in 1596 and which ends with the words which I translate as follows:

"*Laus Deo*. The transcribing of the foregoing was finished Saturday, October 26, 1596, in Seville."

The copy I have was made from the copy in the Lenox Library.

Professor Wright is in error in stating that New Mexico was discovered by "Stephen Dorantes." Stephen and Dorantes were two distinct persons and were slave and master. The four individuals who survived the ill-fated expedition of Panfilo de Narvaez and eventually reached the city of Mexico were Alvar Nuñez Cabeza de Vaca, Andres Dorantes, Alonzo del Castillo Maldonado, and the Negro

Stephen. There was a fifth, who escaped the shipwreck and was afterward found by De Soto, living with the Indians.

Viceroy [Antonio de] Mendoza, writing to the Emperor, Charles V, December 10, 1537, says:

"Cabeza de Vaca and Dorantes, after having arrived here, decided to go to Spain, and knowing that if Your Majesty should be pleased to send the people to that country to ascertain what it really was, there would be no person who could go with them or give them information, I bought of Dorantes, for this purpose, a Negro who came from there and was with them all along, whose name was Stephen, because he was a person of intelligence."

These four men wandered through what is now Texas, turned south and west through the present Mexican states of Chihuahua and Sonora, and reached San Miguel de Culiacan in New Galicia, now the capital of the state of Sinaloa, in April, 1536. From there they proceeded to the city of Mexico and gave the Viceroy an account of their wanderings and what they had seen and heard of a wonderful country to the north and northwest. The Viceroy bought Stephen from Dorantes. Cabeza de Vaca went to Spain and wrote an account of his wandering and, in 1540, was made Governor of Paraguay. Andres Dorantes and Alonzo del Castillo Maldonado disappear from the stage entirely and neither of them ever saw either Arizona or New Mexico.

The Indians who had followed Cabeza de Vaca to Mexico were kept there and trained as interpreters. Stephen himself knew something of their spoken language, was skilled in the use of the sign manual, knew how to deal with them, and was recognized by the Viceroy as a valuable and indispensable part of any expedition that might be sent to explore the unknown country.

Viceroy Mendoza having decided to send an expedition into the new country to verify the reports of Cabeza de Vaca, selected Friar Marcos de Niza as leader of the expedition and sent him to Culiacan, in New Galicia, along with Francisco Vasquez de Coronado, the new Governor of that Province. He was also accompanied by two other friars, the Negro Stephen, and the Indians who had followed Cabeza de Vaca to Mexico.

The expedition to explore the new country left Culiacan March 7, 1539, and was composed of Friar Marcos de Niza, Friar Onorato, the Negro Stephen, the Indian interpreters and many natives from the villages near Culiacan. Friar Onorato was taken sick and left at Petatlan. The expedition reached Vacapa, which Mr. [Adolphe Francis Alphonse] Bandelier[5] has identified as Matape in central Sonora, Friday, March 21, 1529.

From Vacapa Stephen was sent ahead toward the north with instructions to report to the Friar whatever he discovered of importance. He left Vacapa after dinner on Passion Sunday, March 23, 1539. Four days later he sent back a message with a report of what he had heard of the country ahead of him. Castañeda charges that Stephen was sent ahead because he and the friars did not get along well because he was too eager in collecting valuables and because of his immoral relations with the women he met on the way. It is worthy of note that Friar Marcos says nothing of all this in his narrative. Castañeda got his information from the Indians and they no doubt made that charge to excuse themselves to Coronado for having killed Stephen.

I translate as follows a portion of Chapter 2 and all of Chapter 3 of the narrative of Pedro de Castañeda of Najera, chronicler of the Coronado expedition, which left Compostela, in the present state of Jalisco, Monday, February 23, 1540:

"It happened about this time that there arrived in Mexico three Spaniards whose names were Cabeza de Vaca, and Dorantes, and Castillo Maldonado, and a Negro, who had been lost in the fleet which Panfilo de Narvaez took to Florida. They came out by way of Culiacan, having crossed the country from sea to sea, as those who desire to know will find in an account written by Cabeza de Vaca himself and addressed to Prince Philip who is now King of Spain and our Lord. They reported to the good Don Antonio Mendozo how they had, in the country they had crossed, heard and been informed of some powerful villages, four and five stories high, and other things very different from what appeared to be the truth. The good Viceroy communicated this to the good Governor, which was the reason why he hurried, abandoning the tour of inspection he had on hand, and took his departure for his seat of government, taking with him the Negro who had been sold and three friars of the order of St. Francis. One of them was named Friar Marcos de Niza, a theologian and a priest, and another Friar Daniel, a lay brother, and the other Friar Antonio de Santa Maria. As soon as he reached the Province of Culiacan, he at once sent off the friars just mentioned and the Negro, whose name was Stephen, to go in search of that country because Friar Marcos de Niza preferred to go there and see it, as this friar had been in Peru at the time Don Pedro Avalardo went there overland. After said friars and the Negro Stephen had gone, it appears that the Negro did not get along with the friars because he carried along the women that were given to him and gathered turquoises and a collection of everything, and even the Indians in those settlements through which they went got along better with the Negro as they had seen him once before. This was the reason they sent him ahead to open the way and pacify the Indians, so that, when they arrived they would have nothing more to do than keep an account of what they were seeking."

Chapter 3. How those at Cibola killed the Negro Stephen and how Friar Marcos returned in flight.

"As soon as Stephen had left, said the friars, he determined to earn all the reputation and honor for himself, and that the boldness and daring of having alone discovered those villages of high stories so much spoken of throughout that country should be attributed to him. Carrying along with him the people who followed him, he endeavored to cross the wilderness which is between Cibola and the country he had gone through. He was so far ahead of the friars that when they arrived at Chichilticallii, which is on the edge of the wilderness, he was already at Cibola which is 80 leagues of wilderness beyond. From Culiacan to the edge of the wilderness there are 220 leagues and across the wilderness 80, which makes 300, possibly 10 more or less, I think. When the Negro Stephen reached Cibola, he arrived loaded with a great number of turquoises which the Indians had given to him and several beautiful women who also had been given to him and were carried along by the Indians who accompanied him and followed him from all the settlements he had passed. [They] believed they could traverse the whole country without any danger while going under his protection. But, as those people of that country were more intelligent than those who followed Stephen, they gave him lodging in a certain hut they had outside of the village. The elders and those who governed heard his statement and endeavored to learn the cause of his coming to that country. When they were well informed thereof, they deliberated over it for the space of three days. As the Negro informed them that two white men were coming behind him who had been sent by a great lord and knew about the things in the sky and that they were coming to instruct them in divine matters, they concluded that he must be a spy or guide for some nations who intended to come and conquer them. It seemed to them unreasonable for him to say that the people were white in the country from which he came, being black himself and sent by them.

"They went to him and as it seemed hard to them, after further conversation, that he should ask them for turquoises and women, they determined to kill him. [They] did so, but did not kill any of those who went with him. They kept some boys and allowed the others, some 60 persons, to return freely to their own country. As these latter were returning in flight, badly frightened, they happened to come upon and meet the friars in the desert 60 leagues from Cibola. [They] told them the sad news and put them in such fear that, not yet trusting these people who had gone with the Negro, they opened the packs they were carrying and distributed among them everything they had brought with them until nothing remained except the vestments for saying Mass. From there they turned back and traveled by double marches, ready for every emergency, without learning more of the country than what the Indians told them."

The village reached by Stephen has been identified by Mr. Bandelier as Hawikuh of the Indians and Granada of the Spaniards. It is now in ruins, is some fifteen miles southwest from the present village of Zuni and but a short distance within New Mexico, east of the boundary line between that Territory and Arizona. As Friar Marcos came from the

Southwest and turned back in flight when 60 leagues from Hawikuh, it is apparent that he did not enter New Mexico at all and did not see any of the "cities of Cibola." He returned with Coronado the following year and then for the first time saw Hawikuh, July 7, 1540. From there he returned to Mexico, August 3, 1540. Friar Marcos de Niza was the first white man to enter Arizona, but Stephen the black man, entered both Arizona and New Mexico before any white man and the honor of discovering them indisputably belongs to him.

On the 9th of May, 1540, Hernando de Alarcon, under orders of Viceroy Mendoza, sailed from the port of Acapulco on the west coast of Mexico and explored the coast as far as the mouth of the Colorado River, some 60 miles below the present town of Yuma, Arizona. On 26 of August of the same year, he proceeded up the river with about 50 men in two boats. After traveling several days he found a man who had been to Cibola. This man told Alarcon, among other things, that the Head Chief of Cibola had a dog and some dishes he had obtained from a black man who wore a beard and who had been killed at Cibola. [He] later gave more of the particulars of the killing of the Negro. Alarcon had at least one Negro slave with him.

There are several accounts of how Stephen met his death and the Zuni Indians of today have several traditions of the incident. Castaneda [sic] does not say how he was killed. One of the traditions is that Stephen was not killed at all but was taken out of the village at night and given a powerful kick that sent him back to the place from which he came.

Coronado, in his letter to the Viceroy dated at Hawikuh, August 3, 1540, says:

"The death of the Negro is perfectly certain because many of the things he wore have been found, and the Indians say that they killed him here because the Indians of Chichiticalii said he was a bad man, and not like the Christians. [They say] the Christians never kill women but he killed them. He assaulted their women whom the Indians love better than themselves."

It is not my purpose at this time to discuss the killing of Stephen, but I shall reserve that for another place and occasion. I do not believe the charges made against him are true and I shall endeavor to disprove them as soon as I receive certain documents I have ordered from Spain and Mexico. Their truth or falsity, however, in no way affects the issue I am discussing and there is no possible doubt that the Negro Stephen was the first foreigner to tread upon what are now the Territories of Arizona and New Mexico. To him belongs the honor of having discovered them.

Nothing is known of his early history except that he was "black" and a "person of intelligence," in the language of the "good Viceroy" Antonio de Mendoza.

The discoveries of Friar Marcos de Niza, Stephen and Coronado produced no important results and seem to have been forgotten for full forty years. No other expedition was sent into the country to further explore it or to make any use of what had been discovered till 1582, when [Antonio de] Espejo led an expedition and rediscovered the country, as it were.

I will close this article with the following translation from Chapter 8, Part 2 of Castañeda's narrative:

"And here in this Province (then Quirvira, now Kansas) there remained a friar whose name was Juan de Padilla, and a Spanish-Portuguese, and a Negro, and a half breed and certain Indians from the Province of Capotan in New Spain."

So we see there were Negroes in Florida, Texas, Arizona, New Mexico and Kansas nearly a century before the Anglo Saxon set foot upon the North American continent, for [Sir Francis] Drake was not born till 1540.

4

LEGEND OF THE BLACK ROBIN HOOD OF THE BORDERLANDS
Henry Flipper and Pancho Villa

[It was during the Mexican Revolution that raged from 1910 to 1921 that Henry O. Flipper's name became entangled with a bizarre myth concerning General Francisco "Pancho" Villa. As early as 1913, the flamboyant Mexican revolutionary leader was being publicized as a Latin American Robin Hood by his Mexican and American admirers along both sides of the international border. Some of the American war correspondents covering Villa's campaigns, notably the widely read Floyd Gibbons and the brilliant young radical, John Reed, added a professional flair to the publicity that was creating Villa's emerging public image. Villa's pre-Revolutionary feats in banditry and his poverty-stricken childhood seemed to add authenticity to the Robin Hood mythology. His popular image continued to inflate from the heroic "Centaur of the North" to the mythic "Robin Hood of the Rio Grande." The idea proved so appealing to the common man in both Mexico and the American Southwest that it quickly became part of the folklore of both countries, was to inspire several Mexican and Hollywood motion pictures, and remains popular today on both sides of the Rio Grande.

As the Mexican Revolution degenerated into a savage civil war, anti-Villa elements sought to discredit him, particularly among white Americans, by claiming that Pancho Villa was actually of Caribbean African ancestry. In the racist slang of the borderlands, it was alleged that he was really a "Carib nigger." As this tale spread, it gained an air of credibility from eyewitness descriptions of Villa, including some by Americans, that asserted he possessed such Negroid features as thick lips and kinky hair.[1] Other descriptions, which contradicted the former, were ignored by those who were racially biased. The yarn appeared in some American newspapers, one of them as far distant from the Rio Grande as Memphis, Tennessee.[2] By 1918, even the world's foremost scholarly authority on the mulatto, Edward B. Reuter, was declaring that Pancho Villa "seems" to have "some intermixture of Negro blood."[3] As late as 1933, H. H. Dunn, an American biographer of the celebrated Mexican revolutionist, Emiliano Zapata, accepted and perpetuated the story of Villa's partially black heritage.[4]

Meanwhile, Henry Flipper's civilian career as a mining company official and his independent practice as a mining and civil engineer took him to regions within the sphere of Pancho Villa's military and political activities. Flipper became a very familiar figure in several cities and towns of northern Mexico. His professional skills earned him some local prominence in the American border communities of El Paso, Texas, and Nogales, Arizona.

In the rest of the United States, including America's segregated black communities, occasional newspaper articles kept appearing over the years purporting to be authentic accounts of Flipper's frontier exploits. Most of these reports were inaccurate and sensationalized. They usually assumed that his Army dismissal was completely justifiable and often, by innuendo, that he was an unprincipled venturer in civilian life. Nevertheless, some black Americans, especially those in Flipper's hometown of Atlanta, Georgia, were impressed that a black man, born in slavery, was depicted as living a life that to them, in their severely restricted social environments, seemed one of unfettered freedom and bold adventure on a distant and romanticized frontier.

In 1916, a band of mounted Villistas crossed the border and staged a bloody raid on the town of Columbus, New Mexico. This outrage forced President Woodrow Wilson to abandon his cautious policy of "watchful waiting" regarding the violent chaos in Mexico that was threatening American lives and damaging American economic interests south of the border. Wilson ordered a strong punitive expeditionary force, under Brigadier General John J. "Black Jack" Pershing, to intervene in northern Mexico with the mission of pursuing and defeating Pancho Villa and his insurgent forces.

Americans of all races suddenly took an increased interest in the Mexican Revolution when American soldiers became involved in the fighting. African Americans soon heard, with pride, that the Tenth Cavalry, one of the Regular Army's four black regiments, was winning local victories in combat against Mexican troops. Those blacks who recalled Flipper's aborted military career remembered that this was the regiment from which he had been dismissed in disgrace by a court-martial tribunal of white officers.

On July 31, 1914, an event occurred that was to interweave Henry Flipper in a strange and spurious black folktale involving himself and the spectacular General Pancho Villa. On that day, there appeared in the *Boston Advertiser* an article with a headline blaring: "BRAINS BACK OF VILLA. A NEGRO GRADUATE OF WEST POINT SAID TO BE THE RIGHT-HAND MAN OF THE CONSTITU-TIONALIST LEADER." The article claimed that the United States War Department believed that Flipper had become Villa's principal military advisor and that "whatever successes Villa has had in a military way are declared to be due to Flipper."[5]

Flipper was understandably incensed by these outrageous allegations. He decided, however, not to dignify the charges by publishing a denial. Nevertheless, on August 14, 1914, he did vent his reactions in a letter from El Paso to his frequent benefactor, Senator Albert B. Fall of New Mexico, then serving at his post in Washington, D.C. Flipper denied having ever seen Pancho Villa and justly condemned the military advisory tale as "a pure and gratuitous fabrication." He denounced Villa's political motives and charged that "the revolution he is carrying on is one of loot and revenge and has nothing else in view, however loud he and his may prate about the regeneration of the country."[6]

The virus of nationally spread false rumors continued to plague the hapless former officer. On March 18, 1916, there appeared in *The Washington Eagle*, a prominent African American newspaper published in the nation's capital—even then a city of predominantly black population—a front page article headlined: "COLORED

Pancho Villa (center) is flanked by Generals Alvaro Obregón and John J. Pershing. Behind Pershing is a youthful Dwight D. Eisenhower (Arizona Historical Society, Tucson).

ARTILLERYMAN WITH VILLISTA FORCES. DISPATCHES FROM FRONT SAY FLIPPER IS IN MEXICO." This article repeated the saga that former Lieutenant Henry O. Flipper was serving as an officer with Pancho Villa's forces in Mexico and was a military advisor to Villa. Furthermore, it added a new and pernicious charge that Flipper harbored a bitter hostility toward the United States government because of his dismissal from the Army. This allegation was particularly ironical. The 1914 *Boston Advertiser* article claimed the war department believed that Flipper, "the brains back of Villa," was steering the Mexican leader toward a pro-American policy in hopes of reinstatement in the Army.

This time, Flipper, still working in El Paso, fought back publicly. On May 4, 1916, he fired off a blistering and factually detailed denial to *The Washington Eagle*, which the newspaper published on its front page on May 13, 1916. His anger exploded eloquently when he closed his letter with the accusation that the author of the unsigned article "is a conscienceless, gratuitous, malicious, unmitigated liar! His only excuse, if any be admissible, is his superlative ignorance." Regardless of Flipper's protest, the rumors of his involvement with the Villistas persisted and were circulated among black communities throughout the nation.

There can be no doubt about the honesty of Flipper's adamant rejection of Villa's cause in both of his letters and his approval of Pershing's Punitive Expedition in his reaction to *The Washington Eagle* article. Except for the hope of equal opportunity in his Army career and the humiliation of its outcome, Flipper was surprisingly and consistently conservative in his political and economic views. Despite his own frustrations, he remained a gradualist in his outlook on race relations, holding opinions similar to the moderate positions of Booker T. Washington. Furthermore, in 1916, he was employed on the Mexican border as an analyst of the revolution by Republican Senator Albert B. Fall. Fall had extensive business interests in Mexico that were mortally threatened by the Villistas and all the other numerous rebel factions. In Washington, D.C., the Senator was a strident advocate for American military intervention in Mexico.

To some black Americans, a possible Flipper and Villa connection had a ring of plausibility about it. Villa's movement was internationally recognized as a revolt by impoverished Mexicans of Indian ancestry against wealthy and ethnically arrogant Mexicans of Spanish descent who traditionally treated the mestizo peons as their racial inferiors. Black Americans, like all Americans, had been exposed to the popular media image of Villa as the Robin Hood-like hero of humble origin, the scourge of economic oppression and racial injustice. Then, there were always those intriguing yarns about Villa's African blood to be considered.

The tale of Flipper's collaboration with Villa endured through the years in some black communities. In Atlanta, it eventually reached an ultimate in myth-making folklore among those who did believe it. This is dramatically illustrated by a 1960 interview this editor had with Henry Flipper's sister-in-law, Mrs. S.L. Flipper, a former teacher, in Atlanta.

The elderly lady described how Henry arrived at her home in 1931, mysteriously penniless and without luggage despite a recent well-paid position with an American petroleum company in Venezuela:

"He didn't bring nothin' but himself," she said.

To my inquiry about Henry's connection with Villa, her response was truly epical:

"For many years back here," she said, "we heard that Henry Flipper *was* Pancho Villa!"[7]

The following document is a reprint of the July 31, 1914, *Boston Advertiser* article.]

BRAINS BACK OF VILLA. A NEGRO GRADUATE OF WEST POINT SAID TO BE THE RIGHT-HAND MAN OF THE CONSTITUTIONALIST LEADER

A colored man is said to be the genius or brains making a success of Villa. That Villa recognizes no fear is of course known. His daring is very great. He has a willingness to take instant and broad initiative. Still, he is densely illiterate, which is always a great handicap, but it has at all times been clear that he was proceeding according to enlightened military tactics and the War Department knows how Villa has come by it. The force that is supplying it is a colored man named Flipper, who is a Yankee and even a graduate of West Point, and who has been in the United States Army.

It is said that in mind he was as brilliant a cadet as ever studied at West Point and that he brought his talents into the Army where they were much respected. However, his personal deportment was not of the best and it is asserted that he was cashiered and so became disconnected from the Army. He went to Mexico a soldier of fortune, came to know Villa, and has been his right-hand man since. Whatever successes Villa has had in a military way are declared to be due to Flipper. A daring soul without conscience and remorse met a powerful lot of knowing brains and the two agencies have worked admirably together.

It is said that Flipper is desirous of returning to the United States and being reinstated in the United States Army. His influence over Villa is very great. Perhaps the brains back of Villa are at this minute responsible for the friendly attitude of Villa toward the United States. The War Department believes so.

[The following document is an excerpt from Flipper's August 14, 1914, letter to Senator Albert B. Fall in reaction to the *Boston Advertiser* article.]

El Paso, Texas
August 14, 1914
Senator Albert B. Fall,
Washington, D.C.

Dear Sir:

The clipping herewith . . . was taken from the *Boston Advertiser*. . . . Please read it carefully.

The statement that I have been the military advisor of Francisco Villa is, of course, a pure and gratuitous fabrication. I have known of him for many years, but have never seen him and have never been in sympathy with him, his movements or his aims. The revolution he is carrying on is one of loot and revenge and has nothing else in view, however loud he or his may prate about the regeneration of the country.

I have long since ceased to notice newspaper lies about myself, but this one is particularly disagreeable and annoying. Is it possible that some inkling has got out to the effect that I am trying to get back into the Army, as the article states, and that some enemy has had these lies published in order to prejudice my case?

I thought of asking the *El Paso Herald* to reproduce the article with my denial, the statement that I was contemplating suing the *Boston Advertiser* for libel, and to give both to the Associated Press, but I thought better of it. . . . I should like very much to get a denial before the country, because everyone who reads the article will believe it. From time to time during the last thirty odd years, the American newspapers have had me occupying all sorts of government positions in Mexico. At the beginning I denied them but I finally became hardened and let them pass without notice or comment.

Very truly yours,
Henry O. Flipper

[The following document is a reprint of Flipper's letter to *The Washington Eagle*, written from El Paso in 1916 and now in Flipper's personal military file in the National Archives, Washington, D.C. It tells us much about this remarkable but almost forgotten black figure, his views on Villa and Mexico, his life on the Southwest frontier, and the role of Negroes in the Mexican Revolution.]

Editor, *The Washington Eagle*, El Paso, Texas
Washington, D.C. May 4, 1916

In your issue of March 18th last, you published an article under the caption of "COLORED ARTILLERYMAN WITH VILLISTA FORCES. DISPATCHES FROM FRONT SAY FLIPPER IS IN

MEXICO." This article does me an injustice and I hand you herewith a denial which I trust you will publish in as conspicuous a place as that occupied by the article I am refuting.

The article contains so many glaring falsehoods, it is inconceivable that a man of any intelligence could have written it. I am forced to the conclusion that it was written for the sole purpose of injuring me in some way.

In the first place, there are no "colored artillerymen" in our service and there have been none since the Civil War. A "trooper" and an "artilleryman" are two wholly different things. I do not know Villa or [General Venustiano] Carranza or any of the leaders of the so-called "Revolution" in Mexico. I have never seen either of them nor have I ever had any connection of any kind whatsoever with any of them or with their brigandage, or with the Mexican Government at any period whatsoever.

I know Mexico and the Mexican people thoroughly. I have not lost my five senses or any of them to the extent of taking part in the upheaval in that country. I can conceive of no contingency under which I would fight the United States. I am loyal through and through, because no man born in the United States who knows Mexico and has an atom of intelligence can be otherwise, as between the two countries.

I have been in El Paso, Texas, four years, paid to keep in touch with the situation in Mexico and to study and report on it. I have heard no stories of military operations by colored "troopers" in Mexico nor read any dispatches saying that "Flipper is in Mexico." If any such exist your correspondent fabricated them. The men discharged because of the Brownsville [Texas] affair [in 1906] were not discharged at Brownsville but elsewhere, and they were not troopers but infantrymen and they were not in Mexico.[8] Prior to the break between Carranza and Villa, Carranza ordered discharged from his army the few foreigners [who] were in it and it was done promptly. There was a Negro lieutenant in [General Victoriano] Huerta's army at Juarez. He had never been an American soldier, but was a fugitive from justice and is now in the

Texas Penitentiary, where he belongs. There was a major in Villa's army, a colored man who previously kept a hotel at Torreon, a very fine man, but he is now at his home in the United States. There was also a Negro in [Governor Jose Maria] Maytorena's army in Sonora who operated a machine gun. It was said he was a deserter, but this was later denied.

In all of Villa's campaigns, after the break with Carranza, there were no foreigners, Negroes or others, in either army. At Torreon, Villa's Chief of Artillery was General Felipe Angeles, a Mexican, a former Superintendent of the Mexican Military Academy at Chapultepec. He is now living here in this [El Paso] County. There were no Negroes in the fight at Torreon, in any capacity whatever. On the contrary, several peaceable Negroes have been wantonly killed and robbed by bandits of all factions; for they are all bandits! I personally knew of one Negro who was killed simply because he had eight hundred dollars and the bandits wanted the money.

The writer has two perfect ears. He was never mutilated in the slightest degree by white cadets at West Point, the correspondent of The Eagle doubtless referring to Cadet Johnson Chestnut Whittaker, who was reported to have suffered that indignity after Flipper had been graduated and had left West Point.[9] [Major General] Fred Funston is not a West Pointer, was not at West Point when Flipper was there, and was not even connected with the Army in any capacity at that time.[10] Flipper was never "whipped and stripped," was never "tried by hazers," never sentenced "in a hazing court-martial to have his tongue cut out and ears chopped off." Neither ear was ever cut off nor was he removed from West Point. On the contrary, his career at West Point was practically free of molestation of any kind, being hazed, in fact, far less than his white classmates. He was graduated with honors [Class of 1877] and served five full years as a Second Lieutenant in the 10th U.S. Cavalry.

Every colored person in El Paso knows me and knows that I am not and have not been with Villa. They have seen me on the street and elsewhere in El Paso every day for the past four years.

As to American troops going into Mexico, I am glad they have gone, regret that they did not go sooner, and wish them all possible success. Any aid I can give is at their service, now and always.

The 10th Cavalry and the 24th Infantry of Negro troops are now in Mexico. If you have read the dispatches closely, you have observed that the 10th Horse has had the honor of the first fight with the Villa bandits, routing them completely, killing some sixty odd without a single casualty on their part, after riding 55 miles in 17 hours, living fully up to the traditions of that splendid organization. These men are sincerely loyal and acknowledge no superiors as soldiers.

As to myself, I was railroaded out of the Army in 1882. In 1883 I was employed by an American company composed wholly of southerners and worthy ex-Confederate officers as assistant in the survey of public lands in Mexico, for which they held concessions from the [Porfirio] Diaz government. I did similar work as Chief Engineer for a Chicago company and later for a Galveston, Texas, company, completing the work in 1891.

In that year Congress created the Court of Private Land Claims to determine title to a large number of Mexican and Spanish land grants in several of the Southwestern states. I was then employed by the town of Nogales, Arizona, to prepare its case for presentation to the Land Court. The town was on a so-called Mexican land grant and the people were in danger of losing their homes. The preparation of this case brought me to the notice of the United States Attorney for the Land Court. He had the then Attorney General, Mr. Richard Olney, appoint me a Special Agent for the Department of Justice and assign me to his office. I remained in this position for eleven years until the Court completed its labors.

My duties were to go to Mexico and examine the grants on the ground, make such surveys as I thought necessary, hunt up witnesses, be myself the principal witness at the trial of the cases, hunt up and translate the Spanish and Mexican land laws under which the grants had been made and, in short, prepare the cases for the United States Attorney. In the course of this work I collected, translated and arranged, and the Department of Justice published, a collection of Spanish and Mexican land laws running from the 16th Century to 1853, which collection the Land Court and the United States Supreme Court used extensively in reaching their decisions.

At the conclusion of this work in 1901, I was employed as local engineer by the Balvanera Mining company, a West Virginia corporation of New York capitalists operating in Mexico. This company failed two years later and I was left on the ground as keeper of the company's property. In 1905, the property was sold to the [Colonel William C. "Bill"] Greene Gold-Silver Company, also a West Virginia corporation of New York capitalists, and I was retained as a member of the company's staff in the legal department. This company also failed and its mining properties passed to the Sierra Mining Company in 1908, which company also retained me in its legal department. I am an officer of the company and am representing it here in El Paso. I am watching the situation in Mexico and reporting to the home office at Duluth, Minnesota, and to the General Manager in Pittsburgh, Pennsylvania.

In March, 1912, the company, obeying the orders of President [William Howard] Taft, brought all of its American employees out of Mexico and placed me in El Paso, Texas, in the capacity already mentioned above.

As you see, I have been usefully and honorably employed since leaving the Army, and have not had time to meddle in Mexican politics.

From the foregoing it is evident that the writer of the article, which you have printed, is a conscienceless, gratuitous, malicious, unmitigated liar! His only excuse, if any be admissible, is his superlative ignorance.

Very truly yours,
Henry O. Flipper

5

THE PATH TO CAPITOL HILL

[By 1912, Flipper had earned recognition as an expert in Mexican mining and land law, and his engineering duties with companies controlled by Colonel Bill Greene and A.B. Fall had been expanded to include legal consultation. In that year the violence of the Mexican Revolution prompted President William Howard Taft to urge all companies to remove their American employees from Mexico. As a result, Flipper was transferred from Ocampo, Mexico, to the border city of El Paso, Texas. He was assigned to the legal department of the Sierra Mining Company, a corporation partly controlled by Albert Fall, who organized it and was a major stockholder.[1]

In 1912 Fall was elected to the United States Senate as a Republican from New Mexico. He rose to the chairmanship of an influential Senate committee charged with investigating American foreign relations with revolution-convulsed Mexico. Naturally, he had a vested interest in American policy because of his long and complex business involvement in Mexico. A major part of Flipper's mission in El Paso was to gather information for Senator Fall on developments in insurgent Mexico. This material often attained the level of political and military intelligence information. Ironically, in view of the rumors circulating concerning his alleged leadership role in Pancho Villa's revolutionary forces, Flipper's reports revealed a firm anti-Villista viewpoint. He was also critical of Villa's strongest rival, General, later President, Venustiano Carranza.

As early as February, 1914, Flipper assured Fall that he had never participated in Mexican political affairs despite his strong conservative views. He also gave his mentor a hint of his post-Mexican Revolution career goals and reminded him of the ongoing struggle to cleanse his military record. Flipper's concern with these matters was such that they comprised the opening paragraph of a letter otherwise devoted to analyzing the international political significance of a recent anti-Villista rally in El Paso.]

El Paso, Texas,
February 25, 1914.

Senator Albert B. Fall,
Washington, D.C.

Dear Sir:

I have been very, very careful not to mix in any way in the trouble in Mexico. I am too anxious to return to Mexico to make enemies of Mexicans on either side of the controversy and far too anxious for a successful issue to my Army affair to say or do anything to which the [Woodrow Wilson] Administration or any of its participants or friends might take exception....[2]

[On August 10, 1914, we can see an example of Senator Fall commissioning Flipper for specific intelligence information. The material Flipper provided often proved useful to Fall's Senate committee in its official investigations. More confidentially, it was often valuable to Fall personally in formulating his business strategy and in attempting to influence American policy toward Mexico.]

August 10, 1914.

Mr. H.O. Flipper, 803 1/2 So. El Paso St.,
El Paso, Texas.

My dear Lieutenant:

Your letter to me concerning the situation as affecting Villa-Angeles-Felix Diaz was forwarded to the ranch [in New Mexico] just before I left [for Washington, D.C.]. I read what you had to say with much interest.

Albert Bacon Fall (Center for Southwest Research, University of New Mexico Library).

I wish that you would endeavor to ascertain from as reliable a source as possible, just what the present situation is, what Villa is doing, etc., etc.

I wish you would also ascertain for me If Lazaro Del la Garza is in El Paso or Juarez.

If anything new, or if you can ascertain anything definite of interest as to the situation, wire me fully by night letter, not waiting to write.

Sincerely yours,
ALBERT B. FALL[3]

[Five days later Flipper was able to respond with a typically detailed report.]

El Paso, Texas
August 15, 1914.

Senator Albert B. Fall,
Washington, D.C.

Dear Sir:

It is impossible to ascertain just what the present situation is. It can only be inferred from what is being done and talked of. The papers state that Villa has recruited his army to 50,000 or 60,000 men. This is confirmed by the statement of the Mines Company of America that they have been compelled to close down their operations at Dolores and in Parral because what men they had have quit and joined Villa's army. Mr. M. F. Crosset, superintendent of a mine at Cusihuiriachic, told me only two days ago that he had not lost a single day on account of the revolution, but would have to close down now because his men had joined Villa. He says Villa's recruiting officers in his camp paid a bounty of 200 *pesos* and offered two *pesos* a day for recruits. From other sources I have learned that recruiting has been carried on in the mountain regions in the same conditions. Mr. Crosset was an employee of the Greene Gold-Silver Company and was at Santa Brigida with Norval J. Welsh and afterwards at Ocampo with Robert Stewart Brooks. He is reliable in every way. He further says that the bulk of Villa's army is in the small towns and ranches within a day's ride of the city of Chihuahua with only a comparatively small garrison in that city and a similar one in Juarez, in Torreon and Santa Rosalia, all within easy reach of the railroad.

Villa's agents have been buying uniforms here, one house having a contract for 20,000 of them. Arms and ammunition smuggling has been going on as never before, especially as the smugglers can not be arrested under recent orders, although the arms and ammunition may be seized.

There are all sorts of rumors and reports of contemplated revolts against Carranza. There is here now a Mr. Cirilo Ramirez of Hermosillo, the private secretary of Gov. Maytorena. I have known him since 1891 and he was, at one time, one of the wealthy men of Sonora. He tells me that Maytorena of Sonora and Gov. Riveros of Sinaloa are preparing to rebel against Carranza and the rebellion will be inaugurated shortly by the seizure of Nogales, Naco, Cananea and Agua Prieta, the only points in Sonora held by Carrancistas. He is here in the interest of the movement. He says these governors are working in harmony with Villa, who will join the revolt at the proper time and that they have the support of Mr. [President Woodrow] Wilson. This last statement, of course, is gratuitous and made for the purpose of getting adherents.

Villa publicly stated many months ago that Maytorena gave him the $1,000 gold with which he armed and equipped the nine men with whom he began the present revolution, so that there can be no doubt of their cooperation.

I was informed by a person I consider reliable that Lazaro de la Garza held the position of "Commercial and Financial Agent of [Villa's] the Division of the North" in Juarez until about one month ago, when he was removed and that he is now in the city of Chihuahua but holds no official position so far as is known here.

If anything new occurs or if I learn anything definite regarding the situation, I shall wire you as requested.

Very truly yours,
HENRY O. FLIPPER[4]

[Two months later, on October 6, 1914, Flipper was again supplying Fall with political and military intelligence reports.]

El Paso, Texas, Oct. 6/14

Senator Albert B. Fall,
Washington, D.C.

Dear Sir:

The local papers tell us that Jose Bonales Sandoval and Agustin Perez were tried by a drumhead court-martial and shot at Jimenez a few days ago, the very day I wrote and wired you about Felix Dias [sic] having gone to Chihuahua, Oct. 3d.[5]

My information came from Mr. Perez himself. He was a wealthy hacendado from Coahuila and had had all his property confiscated by the Carranza officials and was here with Bonales Sandoval, who is a relative. He and Sandoval have made numerous trips to Chihuahua and once went down with Villa and Obregón.[6] I had every reason to believe the information reliable and nothing has occurred to contradict it so far, although nothing has been heard from Dias either. Mr. Perez told me that Bonales Sandoval came up on the special train and went back with Diaz to Chihuahua. It may be that the shooting is only stage play and not true.

It is reported here that the Herrera brothers, the Arrieta brothers and Chao with their brigades have declared their allegiance to Carranza and have abandoned Villa. A Villa paymaster tells me that Villa has 52,000 men fully armed and equipped and drilled and under good discipline, while the Carranza troops are little more than undisciplined mobs. He also tells me there are several brigades of Carranza troops who will join Villa at the proper time, in case of hostilities, but which are keeping quiet until that event arises. All the arms, ammunition seized by our troops and other federal officials here from smugglers were delivered to Villa officials last Saturday and amounted to several car loads. Since then six million rounds of ammunition have been received from eastern factories, ordered by Villa, and delivered to him. He is ready to fight and if not hampered by the U.S. will beat Carranza. Carranza's action in asking his officers to decide whether he should resign or not was farcical. He had appointed all of them as well as the governors and naturally they were not going to vote themselves out of their jobs.

There is nothing new here.

Very truly yours,
HENRY O. FLIPPER.[7]

[Flipper felt confident enough about Senator Fall's respect for him that he sought the Senator's personal intervention with the Adjutant General of the United States Army on behalf of an old soldier from Flipper's former regiment. Harrison Rather was a black veteran of the Indian Wars who had been a trooper in the Tenth Calvary. He had served with the Buffalo Soldiers during some of the years when Flipper had been the regiment's only black commissioned officer. In 1916, he was living in El Paso and asked ex-Lieutenant Flipper's help in obtaining replacement copies of his Army discharge papers after a six-month delay in response from the military bureaucracy in Washington, D.C. Flipper obliged by requesting Fall to make a "C.I.," or "Congressional Interest" inquiry to the Adjutant General. Flipper's letter is reprinted below.]

El Paso, Texas
January 9, 1916.

Senator A. B. Fall,
Washington, D.C.

Dear Sir:
    In August of last year Harrison Rather, a discharged soldier of

the 10th U.S. Cavalry, wrote the Adjutant General of the army requesting copies of his two discharges. He was discharged from Troop "I", 10th Cavalry, at Presidio del Norte, Texas, in December, 1881, and reenlisted and was duly discharged from Troop "G", 10th Cavalry, at Fort Thomas, Arizona, in December, 1886. His two discharges were destroyed in a fire here in El Paso in 1900.

Would it be asking too much to request you to remind the Adjutant General of this letter of August 27, 1915, and have him, if possible under the law or the practice of his office, to send copies of these two discharges to Harrison Rather, El Paso, Texas, general delivery?

Thanking you for Mr. Rather and for myself,

I am,
Very truly yours,
HENRY O. FLIPPER.[8]

[In early 1916, as he neared his sixtieth year, Henry Flipper's intellectual nature and analytical mind continued to function productively. His concern with the crisis in America's relationship with Mexico and the growing threat of American involvement in the devastating European war led the old cavalryman to explore the new problems arising in United States military policy as the nation debated the issues of defense preparedness in a world turned suddenly dangerous. The result of his study, enhanced by his West Point education and active Army service, was a completely original and highly radical proposal for the selection, training, and expansion of the officer corps of a United States Army, both active and reserve, that was facing unprecedented challenges.

Despite his fondness for traditional values, Flipper's officer candidate plan was surprisingly egalitarian, especially in the provisions for granting commissions to qualified enlisted men. He felt that the increased incentive for advancement would raise the quality of recruits and improve performance of duties throughout all the ranks. His belief that a "caste spirit" prevailed in the Army because of the dominance of West Point graduates is understandable, considering his social ostracism at the Military Academy four decades earlier. Another unique idea was the suggestion to encourage civilian engineers to take military engineering courses at the Army's advanced technical schools. This would help build a strong reserve engineering corps to meet the new technological demands of twentieth-century warfare.

A request from Fall for his views on a suggested branch of West Point to be established in El Paso gave Flipper the opportunity to submit his proposal to Senator Fall in the hope of consideration by the War Department. Flipper delineated his new concept as follows.]

El Paso, Texas
January 9, 1916.

Senator Albert B. Fall,
Washington, D.C.

Dear Sir:

Among the measures proposed for military "preparedness" in this country is the enlargement of the Military Academy at West Point. There seems to me to be a better method and I take the liberty of suggesting it to you.

The government now maintains the following military schools besides the one at West Point:

1.—The Army War College at Washington, D.C.
2.—Army Service Schools:
   a.—The Army School of the Line, Fort Leavenworth, Kansas;
   b.—The Army Staff College;
   c.—The Army Signal School;
   d.—The Army Field Engineering School;
   e.—The Army Field Service and Correspondence School for Medical Officers;
3.—The Army Medical School, Washington, D.C.;
4.—The Coast Artillery School, Fortress Monroe, Va;
5.—The Engineer School, Washington, D.C.;

6.—The Mounted Service School, Fort Riley, Kansas;

7.—The School of Fire for Field Artillery, Fort Sill, Oklahoma;

8.—School of Musketry, Fort Sill, Oklahoma;

9.—Garrison Schools;

10.—Post Schools for Instruction of Enlisted Men;

11.—Schools for Bakers and Cooks, Presidio, California;[9] Washington, D. C., and Fort Riley, Kansas.

Most of these are post-graduate schools for West Pointers and those appointed from civil life and promoted from the ranks.

In my opinion West Point now produces enough officers for the purely technical departments, such as the artillery, engineers and ordnance. Officers for the purely fighting line do not require so much technical training.

Enlisted men now serve three years in the active line and four in the reserves. I would propose that an accurate record be kept of every enlisted man, his character, education, conduct in the service, fitness to become an officer, etc., etc., and that before passing from the line to the reserves, the commanding officers recommend such men as the records show to be worthy for assignment to the post-graduate schools. Let these men take the prescribed course there and when they have completed it, give the honor graduates commissions in the regular establishment, after the West Point graduates have been placed, and the others in the reserves, in the "continental" army and in the militia. The possibility of becoming officers would doubtless secure a much better class of men for enlistment in the army and make better soldiers of themselves and by their influence on the laggards who could never make anything but privates.

These schools are now open to militia officers, but they should be encouraged to take advantage of them to a far greater extent than they now do. Honor graduates among them might also be given commissions in the regular army, thus encouraging them to take the course.

The civil engineers of the country should be induced to take a course in military engineering in the engineering schools at

Washington and Leavenworth. Many engineer officers will be needed in any future great war.

Finally, specially brilliant graduates of the post-graduate schools may be assigned to the artillery and ordnance and given technical instruction at the artillery school at Fortress Monroe, Va., and in the arsenals and arms and ammunition factories of the government and in handling mines and torpedoes.

In a few years we should have an abundant supply of highly trained officers and, in my opinion, that caste spirit that prevails to so great an extent in an army officered wholly by West Point graduates will have disappeared, which would be no small gain to the army itself and to the country.

Under this plan there will be no need of enlarging West Point or of building a second West Point at El Paso, Texas, as was proposed recently by a visiting Texas congressman. The post-graduate schools would doubtless require enlargement, which should be done only after a previously well thought out plan had been adopted.

Very truly yours,

HENRY O. FLIPPER.[10]

[The year 1919 saw Albert Fall's U.S. Senate committee confronted with increasingly complex matters. The demand for expert translation and analysis of Spanish language documents, Mexican laws and court decisions, and interpreting of Spanish-speaking witnesses exceeded the intellectual and cultural resources of the committee's professional staff. Additionally, there was a pressing need for a staff member with personal experience and knowledge of Mexico's politics, economy, and culture.

In Senator Fall's mind, Henry Flipper's qualifications in all these matters overcame the blemish of a court-martial conviction almost forty years earlier. Furthermore, Flipper had been accepted for employment by the United States Department of Justice subsequent to his military troubles and had proved a highly competent and trustworthy official. Finally, he had successfully held managerial positions as an employee of Fall in the world of private business.

On August 12, 1919, Fall received a letter from former Sergeant Barney M. McKay, a black veteran of the Indian Wars. McKay had been loyally supporting Flipper's efforts for Army reinstatement ever since 1898. Still residing in Washington, D.C., McKay's letterhead identified him as an editor and publisher. He urged Fall to appoint Flipper to the Senate staff position and reminded him of Flipper's earlier services for Fall's mining company. He also pointed out that the Federal position might help influence passage of Flipper's latest Army "relief bill." Particularly provocative was his assurance to the Republican Senator that: "The Colored people of the Country would appreciate the compliment paid to Mr. Flipper to the highest should you find it practical to give him that employment."[11]

During the next two weeks, Fall made up his mind. Flipper was the man for the job. On August 26, 1919, Senator Fall telegraphed the message reprinted below to Henry Flipper at his residential address in El Paso.]

WESTERN UNION TELEGRAM

Washington, D.C. Aug. 26, 1919.

H. O. Flipper,
Care of Lauro A. Guirre,
2930 Nashville St.,
El Paso, Texas.

If you chose to come here and work with committee investigating Mexican affairs and continue with us probably six or eight months here and on border, you can draw on me for one hundred and fifty dollars through District National Bank this city for expense to Washington. Will make salary satisfactory. Answer.

Albert B. Fall.
Official Business.[12]

[It is not known how Sergeant McKay became aware of the available position nor if Flipper learned of it and requested McKay to write the letter of recommendation. It is also unknown if McKay's letter played any role in Fall's decision to offer Flipper the appointment two weeks later. McKay's assertion of "Colored" approval was always welcome news to any Republican office holder because Republicans still coveted the black vote even though most black suffrage was then limited to regions outside the South. That may, perhaps, explain why on August 27, 1919, the day after Fall sent Flipper the job offer, he instructed a staff member, Dan M. Jackson, to acknowledge McKay's communication with a formal, yet cordial letter.]

Mexico - Appl. for appt.
Washington, D.C. Aug 27, 1919

Sergt. B. M. McKay,
1417 17th St., N. W.,
Washington, D. C.

My dear Mr. McKay:

I am instructed by Senator Fall to acknowledge receipt of yours of recent date commendary of Lt. Henry O. Flipper for the position of interpreter.

I am pleased to advise you that on even date hereof Senator Fall has wired Lt. Flipper to proceed to Washington for duty with this committee.

Yours very truly,

DAN M. JACKSON[13]

[Whatever the significance of the McKay correspondence may or may not have been, Albert Fall's offer set the sixty-three-year-old black frontiersman on still another trail in pursuing the lonely adventure that was his life. It was a path that led from the Mexican borderlands to America's capital, to service for the United States Senate and, eventually, the United States Department of the Interior.

The job offer presented Flipper an attractive professional opportunity and a stimulating intellectual challenge. It was especially fortuitous in view of his advancing age. It also provided a chance to expedite his dream of clearing his Army record at a more strategic geographical location. Furthermore, as Sergeant McKay had suggested in his letter to Senator Fall, he would have personal contact with other senators who might become allies in his personal crusade.

Flipper was forced to delay acceptance of the proffered position, however, because of distressing financial circumstances that could not be relieved by Fall's offer of $150 expense money. He felt constrained to wire the Senator on August 27 as follows.]

WESTERN UNION TELEGRAM

EL PASO TEX [AUG] 27 [1919]

HON A B FALL
US SENATE WASHINGTON DC

RELUCTANT TO ACCEPT BECAUSE OF UNFITNESS FINANCIALLY STRAITENED
AMOUNT MENTIONED WILL NOT SQUARE ME HERE AND PROVIDE OTHER NECESSITIES
NO WAY OBTAIN FUNDS PLEASE ADVISE

H O FLIPPER.[14]

[On the following day, August 28, Fall replied to Flipper by telegram. He doubled the expense allowance to $300. He also included instructions that shed more light on the scope of Flipper's projected responsibilities.]

WESTERN UNION TELEGRAM

Washington, D.C.
August 28, 1919.

Mr. H.O. Flipper,
El Paso Texas.

If three hundred dollars is sufficient draw on me for amount and come immediately bringing with you your Mexican files of documents decrees orders, and promulgations from Diaz Regime to present together with any other matter which may be useful to Committee.

Albert B. Fall.
Official Business.[15]

[Flipper's response to Fall's increasingly attractive proposal was one that remains somewhat puzzling. On August 29, 1919, the day after receiving Fall's second telegram, he addressed a letter to the Senator. In it, Flipper explained the reasons why he had fallen into such dismal financial difficulties and described his almost impoverished condition in characteristic detail. He claimed to be so destitute of adequate clothing as to make the performance of his projected duties impossible. Flipper concluded his chronicle of woe by reluctantly declining Fall's offer of employment.]

El Paso, Texas,
August 29, 1919.

Hon. Albert B. Fall,
WASHINGTON, D.C.

Dear Sir:

Your telegram received and given the most careful consideration.

My purely personal situation compelled me to send you the answer I sent. For about a year and a half after I came out of Mexico, the Sierra Mining Company paid me a monthly salary of $100, on which I could easily live. At the end of that time they cut it down to $50 per month. I could manage with that sum until the war began in 1914, when prices of all kinds began to go up and since then it has been impossible to do so and I have steadily been going behind without any visible means of bettering myself. There is no work here I can do and an occasional translation for Mr. Walthall or some one else adds very little to the funds at my disposal.[16] I am wearing the same clothes I brought out of Ocampo in 1912, having never had money enough to buy others. They are worn and threadbare and I am ashamed to appear on the streets. I could not form part of your party unless properly dressed and I would need a complete outfit of clothing, shoes, underwear, etc., in order to be fit to join you in the work before your committee. It is painful to have to tell you this, but it is the simple truth, which you can readily understand, and is the reason for my reluctance to accept your offer or to ask any one for the necessary assistance.

If I can be of any service here, I shall be glad to be so.

Very truly yours,

HENRY O. FLIPPER.[17]

[It is apparent that Albert B. Fall had failed to compensate Flipper financially, to any adequate degree, for his services from 1914 to 1919. The reason for his delinquency and the reason for Flipper's acceptance of such treatment remains unclear. It is clear, however, that Fall was determined to bring Flipper to Washington, D.C., in 1919, whatever might be the cost in advance expense money. By September 2, he had made financial arrangements sufficient to meet the needs of the ex-lieutenant and Flipper had, again, attained a Federal appointment. On that date Senator Fall wired.]

WESTERN UNION TELEGRAM

Washington, D. C. Sept 2, 1919

H. O. Flipper,
El Paso, Texas.

Your wire received. Advise date leaving. Take receipts for expense expenditures.

Albert B. Fall.

Official business A. B. Fall.[18]

[Then commenced a comedy of errors as confusion arose over the transfer of Flipper's sorely needed funds from Washington, D.C., to El

Paso. On September 10, a hard-pressed Flipper had to telegraph his senatorial benefactor.]

WESTERN UNION TELEGRAM

EL PASO TEX SEPT 10 1919

HON A B FALL

US S WASHINGTON DC

NO RETURN FROM DRAFT SENT DISTRICT NATL BANK BY BANK HERE ON SECOND INSTANT PLEASE HASTEN

H O FLIPPER[19]

[The good Senator wired clarifying instructions the next day. He also encouraged Flipper to accelerate his travel preparations, with the impressive admonition that: "You are badly needed."]

TELEGRAM
Washington, September 11 [1919],

H. O. Flipper,
El Paso, Texas

District National advises draft received and paid some days ago. Have bank there communicate with District National by wire for confirmation. Advise when you will start. You are badly needed.

A. B. FALL
Official Business[20]

[Finally, on September 15, 1919, Henry Flipper was able to telegraph a terse message to A. B. Fall announcing his imminent departure from El Paso on the long railway journey to Washington, D.C.]

WESTERN UNION TELEGRAM

EL PASO TEX 15 [Sept. 1919]

SENATOR A B FALL

WASHINGTON DC

LEAVE MONDAY NIGHT VIA SANTA FE AND B AND O
H O FLIPPER.[21]

[Flipper served on the staff of Fall's senate committee from
September 1, 1919, to January 15, 1920; and from February 1, 1920,
to March 3, 1921.[22] Since Flipper did not depart El Paso until shortly after September 15, 1919, Senator Fall evidently back-dated his
appointment to September 1st for extra pay purposes.

During his years in the Senate, the ambitious Fall cultivated a
friendship with the gregarious Republican senator from Ohio, Warren
G. Harding. When Harding became President in 1921, he appointed
Albert Bacon Fall of New Mexico as Secretary of the Interior. On
March 5, 1921, the same day he took office, Fall promoted Henry
Flipper to the post of Special Assistant to the Secretary of the Interior
with a salary of $3,000 per year. Flipper served in that position until
March 4, 1923. During those years he worked under Fall's direct
supervision.[23] On March 4, 1923, A. B. Fall, bedeviled by rumors of
complicity in the emerging Teapot Dome scandal, resigned as
Secretary of the Interior. On the same day, Henry Flipper submitted
his own resignation. Facing unemployment just seven days before his
sixty-seventh birthday, Flipper turned toward yet another frontier.

William F. Buckley, Sr.,[24] was a major figure in the American oil
industry who had been one of Albert Fall's friends for several years.
In 1923, Buckley engaged Flipper as engineering and legal consultant
for his Pantepec Petroleum Company in Venezuela. Characteristically,
Flipper was involved in another pioneering venture because Pantepec
was Buckley's instrument to develop the petroleum industry in
Venezuela. The company published Flipper's translation of *Laws of
Hydrocarbons and Other Combustible Minerals* in 1925.[25] He remained
with Pantepec Petroleum until 1930.

The stock market crash of 1929 severely weakened Buckley's company financially, and it obliterated whatever investments and savings that Flipper had accumulated. In 1930 Flipper returned to the United States. He spent a few months in Washington, D.C., and then journeyed home to Atlanta, Georgia, in 1931.]

6

FLIPPER'S LATER RECOLLECTIONS
and Views on Race and Politics
1936-1940

[Henry Flipper was seventy-five years old when he joined the Atlanta household of his younger brother in 1931. He was to reside there until his death at age eighty-four in 1940. During these years the brother, Joseph Simeon Flipper, was still serving as a Bishop of the African Methodist Episcopal Church. For Henry it was indeed a homecoming because he had not returned to Atlanta since a visit fifty-four years earlier following his West Point graduation. In retirement he led a calm life in sharp contrast to the adventurous past. If his body no longer led what Teddy Roosevelt had termed "the strenuous life," the mind of the old soldier and frontiersman remained on strenuous active duty. His bedroom in the Bishop's house served as his study and office. As late as 1939, with his eighty-third birthday approaching, he was still transacting business pertaining to his former position in the legal office of the Pantepec Petroleum Corporation of Venezuela.[1]

During these last years of his life, Flipper developed a friendship with Dr. Thomas Jefferson Flanagan, a prominent member of Atlanta's black community and an associate editor of the *Atlanta Daily World*, one of the nation's major African American newspapers. He and the normally reclusive Flipper engaged in frequent discussions on current racial and political issues as well as historical topics in the latter's bedroom study. In addition, Flipper would sometimes relate long ago experiences at West Point, in the frontier Army, and during civilian years in the still turbulent Southwest. Characteristically, he would often elaborate on subjects discussed in their conversations by writing detailed letters to Flanagan. Views expressed in Flipper's letters sometimes influenced Flanagan's editorials.[2]

The letters were far from the garrulous reminiscences one might expect from a man in his eighties. They were expressed with a cogency that can best be described as legalistic. Always the perfectionist, the grammar, spelling, and punctuation in Flipper's letters were almost flawless. Each was meticulously typewritten with every page carefully numbered.

They reveal Henry Flipper as a conservative who was a strict constructionist in his interpretation of the Constitution, including issues pertaining to race relations. Despite his years in the West, he remained a southerner at heart and supported the doctrine of states' rights. On these issues he was, paradoxically, an African American Jeffersonian. In letters written from 1936 to 1940, he expressed a strong mistrust of the Democratic Party and an outspoken opposition to President Franklin D. Roosevelt and the policies of the New Deal. Many of Flipper's views presaged the ideas expressed today by such prominent black conservatives as Clarence Thomas, Thomas Sowell, and Walter Williams. Throughout his long life, Flipper's position on the virtues of self-help and gradualism in racial matters resembled those of Booker T. Washington who, like Flipper, was also born in 1856 as a slave in the Deep South.

In the letters, Flipper's analysis of race relations in the United States Army span the period from 1873 to the debate over America's involvement in the Second World War in 1940. His West Point, frontier Army, and southwestern civilian recollections supplement his memoirs of 1916 reprinted in Chapter One of this book.

The Editor thanks Dr. Flanagan for conveying the Flipper letters to him and granting permission to quote from them for publication. Selections from them are published here for the first time.]

* * * *

[In early June of 1936 Flipper turned his attention to the Democratic National Convention in Philadelphia which was in the process of nominating President Franklin D. Roosevelt for reelection to a second term. In a June 6th letter to Thomas J. Flanagan he pro-

Flipper in 1923—age sixty-seven (Fort Davis National Historic Site).

claimed his alarm about the future of black Americans under Democratic party rule. Flipper's position was based on his realization that Roosevelt's New Deal programs depended upon a coalition between liberal northern Democrats and conservative, white southern Democrats in which the latter were permitted to maintain white supremacy in the South without significant interference from northern liberals. He was deeply disturbed by the shift of northern black voters to the Democrats in response to New Deal blandishments. He warned that this trend served to increase the power of Democrat racists in the South. In the same letter Flipper also presented a scholar-like defense of states' rights in opposition to Federalism.]

Atlanta, Georgia,
July 6, 1936.

Dear Mr. Flanagan:

So Senator [Ellison D. "Cotton Ed"] Smith[3] of South Carolina and another Democrat walked out of Convention Hall in Philadelphia because a Negro preacher was making the invocation and Smith again walked out when Representative [Arthur W.] Mitchell[4] began his speech. No, I am NOT a Democrat and wonder how any Negro can be one, so long as the political and economic conditions are such as they are. To elect a northern Democrat is to add strength to southern Democracy. *Timeo Danaos et dona ferentes.* (I fear the Greeks even when they bring gifts. Virgil's *Aneid.*)

Politics are seething and the Negro seems inclined to go over to the enemy, who has never given him anything but has taken from him every right heretofore given him that was within the enemy's reach. What the Negro needs and wants is not a mess of pottage, half a dozen fat offices for as many Negroes, but better political, economical and educational conditions. Given these the Negro will work out his own destiny. The real sentiment of the Democratic south was eloquently expressed by Senator Smith's walk-out from the convention hall. Only he had the courage to express it; the others kept silent in order to inveigle the Negro vote. I for one expect no more for our people than the mess of pottage.

There is one power of the States not often mentioned. A majority of all the States in convention assembled can annul the present Constitution, make a different one or even change the form of government, create a monarchy or empire, a soviet or any other form of government. The Congress can do none of these things nor prevent them. States' Rights, the rights of each and all the States, are the basis, the very foundation of our government, not something peculiar to the south but to all the 48 States.

The four [black] graduates of West Point, in their order, are Flipper, John [H.] Alexander, [Charles] Young and [Benjamin O.] Davis [Jr.]. Alexander died shortly [actually seven years] after graduation.[5]

So our [Georgia Governor] Eugene [Talmadge][6] endorses Senator Smith's walk-out at Philadelphia? I thought so and so does all the South. Few of them have the courage of Smith or Eugene. The very few who do not endorse it, such as Anderson of the *Macon Telegraph*, are the exceptions that prove the rule. I can visualize [James A.] Farley[7] saying to the southern delegates: "We are not interfering with your niggers down South; we do not need their votes as you are solidly Democratic and will keep them from voting for any other ticket. We DO need the niggers' vote in New York, Pennsylvania, Ohio, Indiana and, above all, in Illinois and that is what we are fishing for. Don't mind a few niggers in the convention; we have to give them a sop now and then." Every northern Democrat sent to Congress strengthens the Democracy of the South and they will do nothing to change conditions there nor would the Republicans. Southern representation can be reduced under the XIVth Amendment but it would be a difficult problem, a problem of doubtful wisdom and produce the contrary of what would be sought, *ad contraproducentem*. In a word it would be coercion and I am unalterably opposed to coercion in any form. Time and time only can solve the problem and produce more Anderson's of the *Macon Telegraph*. Our great problem is nearer home, the improvement of the condition of our people, the submerged, ignorant masses, a job for the churches, lodges and other agencies. Comparatively few of us are civilized whereas all ought to be.

No, I am NOT a Democrat, not till the South learns what democracy is and stops parading under a name that does not belong to it. Of course, if conditions were as they ought to be Negroes would split just as whites do, because this party represents his political views better than that one does but that millennium is still a long way off. We ought, however, to strive for it. No Negro who knows the condition of his race can conscientiously be a Democrat. There are times when every Negro should vote the Democratic ticket: When only two Democrats are running, he should vote for the best of the two. He should always preserve his right to vote. The other time is when a Democrat is running against a lily-white,[8] who is a stench in the nostrils of all good people.

I have talked myself out of words and here end this missive.

Very truly yours,
HENRY O. FLIPPER.[9]

[Even in his eighties Flipper took justifiable pride in his erudition. Thus, it was not unusual for him to enrich his correspondence with Latin phrases and quotations as illustrated by the sentence from Virgil in the letter above. In a 1931 letter to a former business associate in Venezuela, he recommended Edward Gibbon's *Decline and Fall of the Roman Empire* as "a monumental work."[10]

In a July 9, 1936, letter to Flanagan, West Point's first black graduate reacted skeptically to the nomination of four black alternate candidates for West Point and Annapolis by Democratic Congressman (later Senator) Thomas C. Hennings of Missouri.[11] He also expressed criticism of the quality of American schools in 1936 that are still being widely voiced six decades later.]

Atlanta, Georgia,
July 9, 1936.

Dear Mr. Flanagan:

I am enclosing a clipping from *The Call* of Kansas City, Missouri. It is interesting and will catch Negro votes galore. But let's analyze it. The appointees are white and the alternates Negroes. If one or more of the appointees fail to pass the entrance examination, then one or more of the alternates will try to pass it. But you may be sure the white appointees will pass. Care has undoubtedly been taken to see that they do pass, by coaching and otherwise. But the nomination of Negro alternates will get the Negro vote. Our poor brothers have little or no imagination and learn little or nothing from observation or experience. Watch this item of news and see what the outcome will be. In November the brother in his district will vote *en masse* for Congressman Thomas C. Hennings while none of the four alternates will enter either West Point or Annapolis. I hope I shall prove to be a prophet without honor in my own country.

* * *

No civilized people is so ignorant of their Constitution and functioning of their government as the American people, and this ignorance runs all the way from the college graduate to the most illiterate clodhopper. In our schools, of which we are so justly proud, we are taught everything except the language we imagine we speak and the Constitution of our country. What a vast field for all the "isms" ever dreamed of!

With kindest regards, believe me,
Very truly yours,
HENRY O. FLIPPER.

To Thomas J. Flanagan,
165 Ashby Street, N.W.,
Atlanta, Georgia

[As revealed in the preceding letter, Flipper in his old age reflected a sense of intellectual elitism that was, in that respect, a departure from the philosophy of Booker T. Washington. It was more akin to the concept of W. E. B. Du Bois, Washington's principal adversary, of the

"Talented Tenth" of black intellectuals who would lead the black masses to a higher level of culture. Naturally Flipper never embraced Du Bois' civil rights activism nor his later Marxist radicalism.

In a letter of October 22, 1936, Flipper reiterated his view that black Americans should abandon any allegiance to the Democratic party. He also treated Thomas Flanagan to a display of his erudition in early American political history.]

Atlanta, Georgia,
October 22, 1936.

My dear Mr. Flanagan:

Your editorial in The [Atlanta Daily] World of October 22d is to the point. A free citizen always has the right to choose his political party. The right is personal, natural and inalienable and cannot be restricted except by oppression. The oppression exists in our case. In view of that oppression, I, personally, do not believe the time has come for the Negro to choose to be a Democrat. The party is dominated by that section of it which is responsible for that oppression of the Negro and the Negro should do all in his power to keep that section out of the saddle. It is not human nature to appeal to an avowed enemy for succor.

I think you are in error in crediting Thomas Jefferson with creating the Democratic party, although that is the common belief. Just returning from Minister to France and full of the republican ideas of the revolutions of 1793, he preached democracy or republicanism, which, at that time, was the same thing, and became the head or leader of the Republican party against the other party (Hamilton's) called the Federalist. Indeed, "Republican" was the word most used at that time, "Democrat" had not become fashionable.

Jefferson ran for President on the Republican ticket and was elected [in 1800] as a Republican. Jefferson and [Aaron] Burr received the same number of [electoral] votes, which threw the election into the House. There, through the influence of

Hamilton, the Federalist, the election was given to Jefferson. Both parties, after Jefferson's time, changed their names to Democratic and Whig parties.

With kindest personal regards, believe me,

Very truly yours,
HENRY O. FLIPPER

To Thomas Jefferson Flanagan,
165 Ashby Street, N.W.,
Atlanta, Georgia.

[On February 9, 1937, Flipper wrote a criticism of New Deal welfare programs (usually referred to in the 1930s as "relief" programs) that remarkably foreshadowed the arguments being voiced by welfare opponents sixty years later.

He also presented a conservative critique of the 1930s organized labor movement and its militant tactics. Ever the intellectual, he supported his contentions by quoting Adams Smith's 1776 classic defense of *laissez-faire* capitalism, *The Wealth of Nations*.]

Atlanta, Georgia,
February 9, 1937.

Dear Mr. Flanagan:

Relief cut off, the unthinking mob, whose patriotism is measured by its bellies, will turn against him [President Franklin Roosevelt]. Our method of relief [welfare], considering our dual system of government, was entirely wrong. Instead of giving the President $4,800,000,000 to spend at his discretion and with which to buy votes, that money should have been allotted to the States, on condition that they appropriate an amount equal to their allotment and to take care of their own needy. There would have been some stealing; there was some anyway, but the responsibility would have rested where it belonged, on the States, and the morale of the people would not have been lowered.

As to the "Sit Down" strikers,[12] they are clearly guilty of criminal trespass. They have seized and hold property not their own, thus depriving its rightful owners of its use and enjoyment. Not even the government, Federal or State, can take private property without "due process of law" and just compensation, and no law authorizes a citizen to do so on his own responsibility (Amendments Vth and XIVth). State courts have full legal power to evict them. They are wholly under State jurisdiction. The Federal government has no right to interfere. The Department of Labor has no authority and no power to act in the matter nor in any other. Its function is purely and solely *advisory*. It may give its advice, use its good offices, its influence, but cannot go any further. Strikes like all other activities must be lawful. The law permitting strikes does not permit the unlawful seizure of property nor any other unlawful acts. The law never authorizes a crime. There is among our State authorities a cowardly reluctance to proceed against men in mass—they have votes—and labor is fully aware of this reluctance.

Labor is fast becoming autocratic and tyrannical and some sort of compulsory arbitration will have to be made into law. Adam Smith in his *Wealth of Nations*, London, 1776, says:

"Labour alone, therefore, never varying in its own value, is alone the ultimate and real standard by which the value of *all commodities* can at all times and all places be estimated and compared. *It is their real price.*"

Since the price of labor fixes the price of all other things, the public, the consumer, is interested in that the price of labor be not too high. Labor, if just, will consider not only its own interests but those of the rest of the community. That inordinate thirst for short hours, short weeks and the highest possible wages must be checked by law, if no other ways be offered. Justice should include all people.

* * *

I intended to clip and send you Jacob's last article, but the paper got away from me and I have not been able to find it since nor do I remember the date. Other more careless persons in the house also read the papers and use them for other purposes.

With kindest personal regards, believe me,
HENRY O. FLIPPER

P.S.

The [direct] election of Senators was brought about by amendment [in 1913], of which the mass of the people knew nothing until it was an accomplished fact. So was the change in the inauguration date and meeting of Congress.

Roosevelt has led the people, the unthinking element, to believe the Federal government would take care of them under all circumstances, guarantee them jobs or take care of them when no jobs were to be had, thus lowering their morale.

Old age pensions should come from the State, Congress appropriating funds to aid the States under the welfare clause of the Constitution.

You see, I believe in the States. They existed long before the Federal government, which they themselves made. We do not want a strong central government in this country. History has shown the numberless evils of such government. Every new amendment, like the Child Labor Amendment, weakens the powers of the States and strengthens those of the central government. Amendment is sometimes necessary but it should not be made at the behest of every pseudo reformer who shows his head.

H.O.F.

[Flipper's commitment to the conservative doctrine of states' rights, so clearly expressed in the closing paragraph of the preceding letter, was so firm that he even opposed the efforts being made in the 1930s to enact Federal anti-lynching legislation. He explained the reasoning behind his surprising stand on this controversial issue, a cause so avidly supported by America's black leadership, in an April 6, 1937, letter to Flanagan.]

Atlanta, Georgia,
April 6, 1937.

My dear Mr. Flanagan:

I am amazed at the amount of work being done by the NAACP to get an anti-lynching bill through Congress.[13] I do not for a moment believe any such bill will ever be passed. There is now no political reason for its passage, no election pending, and no occasion to buy votes. I am opposed to a Federal anti-lynching law, because I am convinced of its unconstitutionality. Its primary purpose is to coerce the South and coercion is always a failure. Nothing is more true than the homely aphorism that one can lead a horse to water but can not make him drink. Reconstruction bitterness is gradually though slowly dying out. An anti-lynching law will revive much of it and the Negro will be the loser. All history teaches the futility of coercion. There is an all too common belief among Negroes that the southern white man must be coerced. Coercion kept Ireland Catholic and without it she would have become Protestant like England and Scotland and been pro-British today. The idea of a Federal court trying a county for any reason whatever is not consonant with our theory of local self-government. A State can do that, because it creates the county and prescribes its functions. The Congress has no power to interfere in purely State functions, one of which is to try murder cases, lynchings.

With kindest personal regards, believe, me,
Very truly yours,
HENRY O. FLIPPER.

To Thomas Jefferson Flanagan,
165 Ashby Street, N.W.
Atlanta, Georgia.

[On July 3, 1937, Flipper wrote an authoritative account of the Democrat's white primary election system in Texas and the historic effort of Dr. L.A. Nixon, a black civil-rights pioneer in El Paso, to nullify it. Consistent with his own views, Flipper regretfully concluded that such state restrictions on voting rights were technically constitutional. He also introduced his opinion that state poll taxes were constitutionally legal.

Citing events in recent Texas political history, Flipper clarified further his ideas about the black voters' relationship with the Democratic party.]

Atlanta, Georgia,
July 3, 1937.

My dear Mr. Flanagan:

Have you ever given any thought to what is known as the "White Primary," which exists, I believe, in all the states of the far south?

Texas had a law abolishing nomination by convention, establishing therefore the system of primaries and specifically excluding Negroes from voting at the primaries of the Democratic party. A Dr. [L.A.] Nixon, a Negro physician of El Paso, Texas, turned Democrat, questioned the constitutionality of this law and succeeded in having it declared unconstitutional by the Supreme Court of the United States. That part of the law excluding Negroes became ineffective, so that there is nothing in the statutes of Texas that in any way affects the Negro as a voter in contradistinction to any other voter. But the Democratic Central Committee of the state at once, by resolution, excluded him from the Democratic primaries. Nixon continued his fight, but has lost in every instance. There is nothing of which courts, either state or Federal, can take cognizance. The Democratic Central Committee is not a legislative body; it can make no laws a court is bound to consider. If you attempt to join the Masons and they black-ball you, you have no remedy. You cannot go into court and pray the court to compel them to admit you.

Is there no remedy in law? That is a hard question to answer, but I am of opinion there is none and that there can be none, unless it come from the Democrats themselves. Further, I believe the Democratic Central Committee is in its rights and can exclude whomsoever it pleases. A political party is the people, or a considerable portion of the people, exercising their original inherent, sovereign powers, superior to all governments and rulers, because they make both, are the source of all power. It may do what it pleases. In the old convention days it is certain no Negro would have been elected a delegate to a Democratic nominating convention and none were ever so elected.

As a matter of policy I think the practice of the Democratic party a grave mistake and it should be fought with all the weapons that can be devised.[14] In such states the Negro should be anything but a Democrat. He has never made a greater blunder than to ally himself with those who have systematically deprived him of every right that was not rigidly guarded by law they could not override. He is thus clearly warned not to be a Democrat.

There are occasions where the Negro can and should vote the Democratic ticket, which would not make him a Democrat. When Ma Ferguson was elected Governor of Texas, one of her first acts was to pardon a hundred or more convicts, most of them Negroes. She was severely criticized, but she boldly met her critics and told them she had personally investigated each and every case and that any jury and judge that would sentence a Negro or anyone else to the penitentiary for twenty years for stealing a chicken, not worth more than fifty cents, deserved the execration of every civilized community and her critics promptly ceased their howl. When she ran the second time, she tied another candidate, making necessary a run-off election. This other candidate, in some of his campaign speeches, had said he wanted no Negro votes and if Negro ballots in his favor were found in the ballot boxes, he wanted them thrown out and not counted. When the day for the run-off election arrived, Negroes all over Texas voted for Ma Ferguson and she was triumphantly elected. Negroes clearly showed their wisdom in this case and without becoming Democrats.

You are aware, of course, that Negroes vote freely in Texas at all elections, if they have paid their poll tax, but never in Democratic primaries, and the poll tax is not unconstitutional.

The foregoing is, perhaps, a bold opinion, but I see no other way out of the dilemma.

With kindest personal regards, believe me,
Very truly yours,
HENRY O. FLIPPER

[It was natural that the discussions between the two friends would turn to Flipper's interesting experiences of many years before. On July 7, 1937, Flipper sent the journalist an account of cadet life at West Point sixty years earlier and a later civilian experience in El Paso, Texas, in 1897. At age eighty-one the old frontiersman still retained detailed memories of his eventful life and, moreover, could write of them with undiminished clarity and logic.

He also used the occasion to reiterate his concern about what he perceived to be a glaring cultural lag among even better educated contemporary African Americans.]

Atlanta, Georgia,
July 7, 1937.

My dear Mr. Flanagan:

At West Point [in 1877] the Corps of Cadets is divided into four companies, each under an Army officer known as "tactical officer." There is also a full quota of cadet officers, captain, lieutenants, sergeants and corporals. Cadets do all their studying in their quarters, two of each class being in each room. The terms senior, junior, sophomore and freshman are never used. The senior class is called first class, the junior second class, the sophomore third class and freshman fourth class. The members of the latter class, in the argot of the Academy, are dubbed "plebes." Each class is divided into sections of eight or ten cadets for recitation. Each cadet has a schedule of his studies and hours for recitation. All recitations are heard in a separate building, known as the Academic Building. The hour for each recitation is sounded by a bugler. The proper sections turn out and are marched to the Academic Building. The instructors are all Army officers and one instructor may hear five or six sections in a day. The Professors go from room to room, listen to the recitation and ask questions. At times a Professor will take the instructor's seat and hear the entire recitation.

This happened once [in 1877] to my section when we were to recite the lesson in Geology and Mineralogy. I happened to be the first or second to recite. After hearing my recitation and asking a few questions, the Professor picked up a rock lying on the desk, handed it to me and said:

"Now, Mr. Flipper, tell us what this is."

I didn't know, any more than the man in the moon, what it was. I turned it over and about and looked long at it and, do you know, it suddenly occurred to me I had seen that very rock in one of the cabinets and the label stood right out before me, before my eyes, so that I could see and read it. I told him what the rock was and then he said:

"That is right. Now tell me how you know it is so and so."

That was a poser too, but I met it and answered:

"I know it is so and so from observation."

He reached for the rock, I gave it to him and he laid it on the desk. He then gave us a lecture on observation:

"The biggest and best school in the world is the School of Observation. If you are duly observant, you will learn more in that school than in all the books you ever study," and so on til it was time to dismiss the section, the other members not having time to recite.

Some twenty years later [1897], in El Paso, Texas, I had occasion to go into a building. As one enters, the elevator is directly in front of him. On the occasion in question there were some ten or twelve persons waiting for the elevator then somewhere up in the building. Among them was the city detective, whom I knew very well. He stepped up to me and asked how high up I was going. I told him that I was going to the second floor. He said:

"I am too. Come on. We can walk up before the elevator gets down."

We walked up and at the top he stopped and asked me:

"How many steps did we come up?" I replied:

"I don't know. I didn't count them."

"Well, you ought to have counted them. That information may never be of the slightest benefit or injury to you, if you live a million years, and yet tomorrow your very life may depend on it. All bankers, merchants, railroad and ship men are always observant, especially of people about them. People, things, actions, and all of the things of life are fit subjects for observation. The immediate importance of counting the steps, however, is to train you to observe."

I am reminded of the foregoing by what follows. During the last three or four months [March through June, 1937, in Atlanta, Georgia], nearly every week, delegations of four or five [black] ministers, some of them with their wives, have motored over from South Carolina to consult the Bishop [Henry's brother, Bishop Joseph Simeon Flipper of the African Methodist Episcopal Church, in whose home the elderly Henry was then residing], and have always had dinner here in the house before returning. It has been a matter of keen interest to me to observe how none of them knew how to use the knife and fork and spoon, thus indicating a similar lack of knowledge of other things that might have been learned by observation, if not otherwise. These men, like Topsy, have grown up in families where no one knew anything different. Grown up now themselves, their children have no other instructor than the example of their parents. It is strange that the subject of observation has never been broached to them, had never even suggested itself to them. The use of the knife and fork is only one of many important things they could have learned by observation. Each now has a church and is trying to lead his people, in some things blindly, because his vision is limited. They see none of the causes and effects that affect their lives so profoundly.

I well remember such occurrences as this at West Point. Some new [white] cadet would be eating with his knife when some older cadet farther along on the table would suddenly jump up and exclaim:

"Look at that Plebe trying to cut his throat!"

Some cadet nearer him would ask: "What are you trying to kill yourself for?"

He would mutter: "I'm not trying to kill myself."

"Then keep that knife out of your mouth! Use your fork."

Or some cadet from the backwoods who poured his coffee into the saucer would be brusquely ordered to pour it back into the cup and to drink it from the cup.

We had a Professor of History and Ethics who lectured us on such topics, but the older cadets, hazing the new ones, soon taught them good table manners.

All high school and college students should be taught to observe. School education at best is narrow and should be broadened by observation, perhaps the only way, and it costs nothing. Each one can easily train himself, but it must be suggested to him, lest, like the preachers, he never have an inkling of it.

At one time I could walk along a street and not only see but perceive everything on the street, on both sides and in the street itself. A glance was all that was necessary to do so. Every person and every thing carries a label and, once we know it, we perceive without trouble or hesitation.

The School of Observation is after all the biggest and best school always.

With kindest personal regards, believe me,

Very truly yours,
HENRY O. FLIPPER

[Even in old age Henry Flipper continued to manifest reactions indicative of the sociologically "marginal man." The previous letter of July 7, 1937, remarking on southern black clergymen's lack of table manners and the August 27, 1937, letter below, reveal his dilemma. He was embarrassed and offended whenever fellow blacks failed to demonstrate cultural levels and traits commensurate with white standards and values. As a culturally marginal man, however, he was likewise wounded and frustrated whenever white individuals or white society denied him equal social status or intellectual recognition. Flipper cast some of the blame for African American cultural lag on curricular deficiencies in the black public schools.]

Atlanta, Georgia,
August 27, 1937.

My dear Mr. Flanagan:

Have you ever noticed anything like this? My Bishop brother receives a rather large mail from his preachers in South Carolina, his present episcopal district, from some in Florida, his former district, and from still others in all parts of the country. Of these letters I see only the envelopes with the addresses they carry. More than fifty per cent of these addresses are written *with pencils* and presumably the letters inside are also written with pencils. The American Negro is possibly the only person in the world who writes his letters with a pencil, not the better educated class but still a large majority of him, man and woman. The Professor of History and Ethics at West Point, in his lectures to the senior class, there called the first class, never failed to characterize this practice as a distinct discourtesy to be avoided. It seems that in our schools little or nothing is taught about letter-writing, at least of the good or bad manners involved in it. I have never received a letter from a white person written with a pencil, but they come written with a pencil from many race correspondents. I do not like it! Behold the observer!

* * *

These are the thoughts of the moment.

Trust you and yours keep in the best of health and with best wishes, believe me,

Very truly yours,
HENRY O. FLIPPER.

[Although Henry Flipper spent his childhood in slavery, in old age he was capable of writing about the South's "peculiar institution" in an historical analysis rooted in his strict constructionist Constitutional philosophy. In a letter of October 18, 1937, he favored T. J. Flanagan with a miniature treatise on slavery and the United States Constitution. His conservative interpretation led him to conclude that the original Constitution contained no prohibition against slavery and that President Lincoln's Civil War actions against slavery were, at that time, unconstitutional. His argument was written in the legalistic manner typical of his early eighties but was, as always, precise and understandable to the lay reader.]

Atlanta, Georgia,
October 18, 1937.

My dear Mr. Flanagan,

Did you read Kelly Miller's[15] well written release on the Constitution in *The World* of October 18th?

He seems to think that Article I, beginning "Migration and importation"; Section 2 of Article IV, beginning "No person held to service or labour" and the last part of Article V prohibiting the enactment of certain amendments before 1808, refer to Negro slavery. I believe he is wrong, at least I hold the contrary view. If Miller is right, the Congress had full power to abolish slavery at any time after 1808, a view never held by anybody, north or south. The slave holding members of the Constitutional Convention saw to it that no such power was given to Congress in the instrument they adopted. Lincoln seized and confiscated the slaves just as he seized and confiscated cotton and other property of those in rebellion against the government, as a war measure, as he had no Constitutional authority for doing so.

Turning back now to Article I, Section 2, clause beginning

"Representation and direct taxes," we find the following four classes of persons:

1. Free persons, to be counted.
2. Those bound to service for a term of years, to be counted.
3. Indians not taxed, not to be counted.
4. Three-fifths of all other persons, to be counted.

It is clear that "three-fifths of all other persons" refers to Negro slavery and just as clear that "those bound to service for a term of years" do not refer to Negro slaves. Who then are "those bound to service for a term of years" or "held to service or labour in any State"? There was a large number of white persons in the Colonies, especially in the north, who were hired out and another number apprenticed for terms of years. They were known as "indentured servants" and were held under indentures or contracts. It was a sort of voluntary-involuntary servitude permitted under English law and that is what the Constitution permitted until 1808 and prohibited after that date. "Migration" connotes voluntary coming and "importation" means only hiring servants under indentures or contracts in England and bringing them over.

It is to be noted that slaveholders never sought the return of fugitive slaves under Article IV, but under specific fugitive slave laws they were expert enough to get through Congress.

To fully understand the Constitution we must know something of the conditions that influenced its framing and adoption.

With kindest personal regards, believe me ever,
Very truly yours,
HENRY O. FLIPPER.

[As 1937 neared its end, the eighty-one year old Flipper turned his attention again to New Deal welfare policies and to the national controversy over state poll-tax laws. In a letter on December 13, 1937, he was passionate in his belief that America was becoming a welfare state in which industry was Federally deprived of its capacity to produce jobs and, ironically, labor was forced on the relief rolls. Flipper discerned what economists and historians were later to discover.

Namely, that after some early economic recovery, New Deal policies began to falter with the nation relapsing into depression again by the close of 1937. He also foresaw the rise in America of a whole new class of welfare bureaucrats.

Additionally, Flipper elaborated previously expressed views that state poll-tax laws were completely Constitutional. He pointed out the little known fact that poll taxes were by no means restricted to the South. In 1937, twenty-six states around the nation still retained the taxes in addition to the eleven former Confederate states.]

Atlanta, Georgia,
December 13, 1937.

My dear Mr. Flanagan:

The New Deal was wrong in its inception, because based on the idea that those who have must support those who have not, with the additional Rooseveltian theory that this must be done through the Federal government, that is, to get the money the Federal government must tax those who have till it hurts and use that money to maintain the shiftless, the lazy and the vice-ridden, not realizing that by depriving industry of its capital to squander on the aforesaid and their white collar distributors, it was depriving industry of the means of employing labor and thus throwing labor itself among those it sought to relieve.

Roosevelt has always been an impractical theorist, idealist and dreamer and was such as Governor of New York [1928-1932]. To have relieved the situation he found [as President in 1933], it would have been advisable to ease the burden on industry to allow it to use the money to employ and maintain the employment of labor. The people at work would have been happy and contented. As it is, its morale has been seriously impaired and we have something we have never had in this country, a recession to a crisis. Heretofore when a panic began it ran its course and disappeared and did not return, but we are now getting back into the depression, a depression of our own and not world-wide. Whatever gains have been made are slipping away.

The Negro voted twice for Roosevelt [in 1932 and 1936]. On neither occasion was his vote necessary. He was elected without it, but the Negro has been a strong factor in the election of Democratic senators and representatives in the North, forgetting that he was strengthening the hold of the Democratic party in the South. What has he received for his infidelity to the god that brought him up out of Egypt? A few unimportant offices, none of them in the South where the mass of his own people live. He has been faithful to his new idol and has received from the South a new Associate Justice of the Ku Klux Klan to pass on his cases, when they reach the U.S. Supreme Court. . . .[16]

I see the U.S. Supreme Court has unanimously upheld the Georgia law requiring payment of a poll tax in order to vote. There are some things in this world of ours so simple it is more than a wonder that some people will not understand them. The vote is not a right or a privilege that one can demand; it is not from the United States but is a gift from the State, which the State can restrict as it pleases or deny altogether for any reason except race, color, previous condition of servitude or sex. Thirty-seven States have poll tax laws similar to that of Georgia. In no State can convicts or the insane vote nor can the officers and men of the Army, Navy or Marine Corps and no one can vote in the District of Columbia.[17]

With kindest personal regards, believe me,
Very truly yours,
HENRY O. FLIPPER.

[By 1939 Flipper was still critical of the NAACP's pro-Roosevelt stance, especially the organization's early support of FDR's reelection to an unprecedented third term in 1940. He also had solidified his convictions that Federal anti-lynching legislation was both futile and unconstitutional. Ironically, he was forced to close his August 12, 1939, letter with comments about a new upsurge of racism in neighboring Alabama. Writing less than a month before the September 3rd outbreak of the Second World War in Europe, Flipper revealed an insight to world affairs, as well as domestic issues, when he combined the two in his analysis of the effects of post-Civil War Reconstruction policies in the South.]

Atlanta, Georgia,
August 12, 1939.

Thomas J. Flanagan,
165 Ashby Street, N.W.
Atlanta, Georgia.

My dear Mr. Flanagan:

The 76th Congress of the United States of America closed its first session August 5th of this year of our Lord, one thousand nine hundred and thirty-nine, leaving the New Deal pretty well shot to pieces and, if not dead, moribund....

It is shocking in this connection to read that the N.A.A.C.P., at so early a date, more than a year before nomination, is advising Negroes to vote for Franklin D. Roosevelt, if he should receive the nomination....

* * *

While in no sense a prophet but sure to be without honor in my own country, it is my deliberate opinion that no American Congress will ever pass an anti-lynching law. Aside from being manifestly unconstitutional, it is ill-advised, impolitic, serving only to intensify racial antipathies. Its avowed purpose is to coerce the South, another "Reconstruction," like that of 1865 and the years following, for the punishment of the white South. While the white South has suffered and is still suffering from the effects of "Reconstruction," not altogether without its own fault, the punishment ricocheted onto the black South and it has suffered most, because a minority without political power, wealth or learning and, therefore, unable to combat it. History shows that coercion is always contra-productive. "Reconstruction" was a failure. England's persecution of the Irish centuries ago has its repercussion in hundreds of the members of the Irish Republican Army in London terrorizing the people with bombs. The coercive clauses of the Treaty of Versailles have given us Adolph Hitler and the consequent unrest in all the world. It must not be thought that the South, the Irish and Hitler are without blame. With us there is far too much emphasis on the word "South."

* * *

Another anti-Negro organization has recently been formed in Alabama under the name of "Alabama Council of Accepted Americans," among whom of course Negroes will not be included. Like the infamous Ku Klux Klan it will tend to keep capital out of the South and thus retard its development and progress.

I trust you and yours keep well and enjoy life.

With best wishes, I am, as ever,
Very truly yours,
HENRY O. FLIPPER.

[Thirty-one days after the start of World War II in Europe, the eighty-three-year-old West Pointer and combat veteran of the Indian Wars was ready to do battle again. He also drew on memories of frontier Army service and his thorough knowledge of the past and current black American military experience to make a specific recommendation regarding the role of black commissioned officers in the soon to be expanded United States Army. Flipper expressed these views with customary vigor and preciseness in an October 4, 1939, letter to Thomas Flanagan.]

Atlanta, Georgia,
October 4, 1939.

My dear Mr. Flanagan:

Another war! What do I think about conditions? It seems to me democracy is in far greater danger now than in 1914. It also seems there are far too much hysteria and emotionalism among the American people. I believe if the war is prolonged, we shall be drawn into it; not only that, I believe we should go in now with all our might. The so-called Neutrality Act should be repealed and we should get back to international law as it existed before hysteria and emotionalism had that law enacted by Congress. Let all nations buy anything they want and can pay for but make them come and get it. We should not deliver.

In the event that the United States get into the war, shall we have a Negro division? No. There is no Negro capable of commanding a division. The men who have commanded divisions in an army have first commanded a company, then a battalion, a regiment, a brigade and then possibly he will be fit to command a division. Many whites failed in the Civil War on both sides. [Ambrose E.] Burnside in the Union Army and [Nathan Bedford] Forrest in the Confederate, both excellent officers within their ability, are good examples.

The foregoing gives me the chance to refer to another matter that does not seem to have occurred to any one else. We have one Negro officer in the Regular Army, Lieut. B.[enjamin] O. Davis [Jr.]. It is my information that he is now at Tuskegee [Institute] playing soldier with a lot of school boys over whom he has no control and can not discipline and is not himself under discipline. He ought to be with his company and regiment, getting experience, elbowing with his captain and first lieutenant and other white officers of his regiment, breaking down prejudice, learning to command his company and preparing himself to command larger bodies, for that is the only way. To keep him away from his regiment in some school or college is to keep him practically out of the Army, although he wears the uniform. When I joined my regiment in the winter of 1878 at Fort Sill, Indian Territory, now Oklahoma, an effort was made to have me sent to a [black] college in Texas.[18] I protested and succeeded in having the President of the college withdraw his application to the War Department and remained with my regiment.[19] On one occasion Troop "G" had its captain under arrest awaiting court-martial, the first lieutenant absent on sick leave and no second lieutenant. I was assigned to command the troop and did so for nearly a year until the captain returned (a company in infantry, in cavalry the same thing is called a troop and in artillery a battery). The routine duties of an officer in a garrison are many. He serves in his turn as Officer of the Guard, Officer of the Day, as member of garrison courts-martial, as member of boards of inquiry, and many others, in which he necessarily rubs elbows with his brother officers, thus wearing down racial prejudice. Lieutenant Davis ought to ask to be relieved of his present duties and returned to his company and regiment.

With kindest personal regards, believe me,
Very truly yours,
HENRY O. FLIPPER.

[Six days later in a letter of October 10, 1939, Flipper returned to the problems faced by black Army officers discussed in his previous letter. Again using the career of young Lieutenant Benjamin O. Davis as an example, he called for action by the African American press to demand that black officers be assigned to active troop duty in the Regular Army's black regiments instead of being relegated to military training instructorships at African American colleges. He sharply criticized the black colleges for cooperating with the War Department in this discriminatory policy.]

Atlanta, Georgia,
October 10, 1939.

My dear Mr. Flanagan:
    You doubtless read an article in the *Atlanta Daily World* on the ill treatment of colored soldiers in our Army and noted the suggestion that colored officers would, in large measure prevent it. This is in line with what I stated to you in my last letter. We have only one such officer who is kept away from his company and regiment to the satisfaction, no doubt, of his fellow officers. He is not wholly to blame; he must obey orders, but the colleges are to blame, in this case Tuskegee. They apply to the War Department to have an officer, in this case by name, sent to the school to train

a bunch of students and the War Department complies. The training he gives is confined to drilling, at such times as the students are not otherwise occupied. Its kind and amount is necessarily limited and is more for show than anything else and is a soft snap for the unambitious officer. If Lieut. Davis himself realized what is happening and his duty to himself, his regiment and his people, he would apply to be relieved and to return to his company and regiment. The [black] colleges should be made to see the wrong they do by taking him from his military duties and should cease to apply for officers. Any sergeant could do what Lieut. Davis is doing and not be missed from his company. A better way would be to drill their students with such means as they now have and each year ask the War Department to send an officer to inspect and report on conditions. The Negro press should take this matter up and see that Negro officers are not nullified by being perpetually kept from their commands.

With kindest personal regards, believe me,
Very truly yours,
HENRY O. FLIPPER

[On March 21, 1940, Henry Flipper celebrated his eighty-fourth birthday. He was unaware, or course, that only forty-three more days of life remained to him. Whatever he may have done on that birthday, he found time to write another letter to Editor Flanagan. In it he made no mention of his eighty-fourth anniversary, but he did set forth his reasons for opposing Federal anti-poll tax legislation more thoroughly than in any previous communication. He combined conservative Constitutional arguments with an original concept that asserted an ethical obligation on the part of low-income citizens, black as well as white, to bear at least a minimum of the public tax burden. He took his fellow blacks to task for denying that obligation in their "whine" against the poll tax. He pointed out again that poll taxes existed in some other states outside the South including even New England. Flipper urged equal funding for the South's segregated black public schools to help produce more black taxpayers in the future.]

Atlanta, Georgia,
March 21, 1940.

My dear Mr. Flanagan:

The poll tax question is to the fore again. Representative Lee Geyer of California has introduced a bill to have Congress wipe out the poll tax everywhere, wherever it exists. He says 3,000,000 Negroes and 4,000,000 poor whites are disfranchised by such laws. I wrote to Washington for information and enclose a copy of the answer I received. I was surprised to find that two of the oldest New England States, New Hampshire and Rhode Island, have poll tax laws and among the highest too. The amount of the tax is insignificant, except in Mississippi, but even that is not excessive when we consider that it is for a whole year. He is indeed a poor specimen of a citizen who can not pay as little as one dollar per year.

In my opinion the Congress has no control over the taxing power of a State. That power is reserved to the States in the Bill of Rights (10th Amendment), because not specifically ceded to the Congress in the Constitution. If there be any discrimination in levying the tax, the courts already have jurisdiction under the XIVth Amendment. They can order the discontinuance of the discrimination, but they can not fix the tax nor fix its amount or sanctions or forbid it altogether.

As my brain sees it, the poll tax laws do not disfranchise any one; they put the decision up to him and let him decide it. He may pay the tax and vote or refuse to pay it and not vote. He franchises or disfranchises himself, not the State. But, if the poll tax be a menace or challenge, why not accept the challenge, pay the tax, get the vote and then use it to elect men pledged to repeal the obnoxious tax?

It seems to me the whine against the poll tax comes with poor grace from the Negro. The amount of the taxes of all kinds paid by Negroes anywhere is insignificant as compared with the total of taxes paid by the whites and this is one reason why teachers of our [black] public schools are paid less wages than teachers doing identical work in white schools; the white tax payer instinctively shrinks from bearing the whole expense of Negro schools as the Negro himself contributes so little. This is a shortsighted view. The State takes care of its insane and they contribute nothing nor should they. It ought also to support its schools, all of them alike, without any ulterior consideration, because an educated citizenry is the highest and best asset any State can have, and such citizenry will ultimately be the best tax payers.

There seems to be much misconception, if not ignorance, of the poll tax. Why should not the man who has no taxable property but enjoys the benefits of government, pay something toward the support of that government? As he has nothing that can be taxed, why should not his person, his head, his poll be taxed? There is no other penalty, no other sanction, than to deprive him of some one of the rights he enjoys without contributing anything to its maintenance or, as was done in Europe at one time, sentence him to serve in the army for such or such time.

* * *

The list I am sending you will make a good item for publication in *The Atlanta World* with comments on the existence of poll tax laws in staid New England.

With kindest regards, believe me,
Very truly yours,
HENRY O. FLIPPER

[During his correspondence with Thomas Flanagan, Flipper often discussed his belief that the Constitution strengthened the doctrine of states' rights rather than weakened that principle. In a letter of March 25, 1940, he developed his theory in its greatest detail. Never one to flinch at the conclusions to which his logic might lead, Flipper posited the provocative view that the legitimacy of a state's secession from the Union had been decided only by military force, and was still undecided as a matter of law. He closed by once more raising a question about the quality of education being provided by black teachers in the segregated black public schools.]

Atlanta, Georgia,
March 25, 1940.

My Dear Mr. Flanagan:

The Federal government, both Congress and the Executive branch, has encroached on the rights of the States from the beginning of the government and even the [Executive] Departments make decisions at times to which they give the effect of law without enactment by Congress or judgment of the courts. The present administration has sinned more than any other. [Secretary of State Cordell] Hull's trade pacts are treaties made without confirmation by the Senate. "He (the President) shall have power, *by and with the advice of the Senate*, to make treaties, provided two-thirds of the Senate present concur;...." The States through their Senators, are deprived of any voice in the making of such pacts, though they are directly affected as to the products they might have for export. Most of the encroachments are made so insidiously they are not noticed, if known, and when known are not noticed, and if noticed an "Oh, well!" is the only attention given to them.

But what are "States' Rights" under the Constitution? They are clearly defined in the Bill of Rights, Amendment X: "The powers not delegated to the United States by the Constitution, nor prohibited by it to the States, are reserved to the States, or to the people." That is clear in connection with the Constitution itself, where the powers delegated to the United States are plainly specified, Article I, Section 8. The Senate is not authorized to delegate its powers. Under the above definition, the anti-lynching legislation, if any, and the Geyer bill to wipe out State poll taxes are clear encroachments on "States' Rights" and therefore unconstitutional, as the Constitution nowhere authorizes the Federal government to sue a county anywhere for any purpose nor to meddle with the taxing power of a State.

In the Civil War period the South claimed the right to withdraw from the Union, a right not even hinted at in the Constitution they had ratified. The abstract question whether a State has the right to withdraw has never been answered except by force and probably will never be answered as a question of right, a question of law.

* * *

The Dean of Howard University [Kelly Miller] says that Negro school teachers know little and care less of the big questions of the day. How about it?

Best regards and good wishes,
Very truly yours,
HENRY O. FLIPPER

[Although the shadow of death lurked only seventeen days away, there was no evidence of that in Flipper's April 16, 1940, letter. It was fitting that his last letter to come to light was essentially a lecture on the importance of accurate usage in the English language and a lesson in its Latin derivation. This was partially illustrated by a precise memory of an 1898 experience. Racially, one of Henry Flipper's last recorded concerns was an admonition to the nation's African American press to become a model of English language excellence for its black readership. Though he had made no mention of his own recent eighty-fourth birthday, the aging frontiersman was thoughtful enough to close his letter with congratulations on the fiftieth birthday of his good friend Flanagan.]

Atlanta, Georgia,
April 16, 1940.

Dear Mr. Flanagan:

A little journey into good English! Do you mind? Notice clippings herewith, Nos. 1, 2 and 3 and their headings. Two read CAPITAL COMMENT and one reads CAPITOL COMMENT.

Nos. 2 and 3 are identical, though the headings are different. Which is right? Which is wrong? Are both right and interchangeable or both wrong?

CAPITOL is from Latin CAPITOLIUM. In ancient Rome the CAPITOLIUM was the Temple of Jupiter and the most magnificent building in that rich and imperial city. Rome itself was the URBS CAPITALIS, the head or chief city of the far-flung Roman Empire. Both CAPITOLIUM and CAPITALIS are from the Latin CAPUT, meaning head or chief. CAPITOLIUM was the head or chief building in Rome while Rome was the head or chief city of the Empire. CAPITALIS and its English derivative are both adjectives and the word URBS or city is always to be supplied or understood. In such case CAPITAL COMMENT is correct and CAPITOL COMMENT is incorrect. The COMMENT is about the city and not the building where Congress meets.

Forty-two years ago—1898—while in Washington [D.C.], I met a young man by the name of [Charles] Alexander. He taught printing at Tuskegee and was in Washington on some business for that institution.[20] He wrote a letter to some friend there giving his impressions of Washington and was kind enough to allow me to read it. He spoke several times of "this CAPITOL city" and I told him CAPITOL was the building where Congress met and not the city, which was CAPITAL. He was much surprised to know there were two words with such different meaning. Now, forty-two years later the same mistake is made and that too by a printer.

Clipping No. 4. This clipping expresses my views exactly. The newspaper and especially the [black] race paper should be a source of instruction, contain the best of good English with, generally, an exclusion of slang and with emphasis on the proper use of words. Many race papers are weak on this point. The race paper should be a virtual text book on orthography, grammar, rhetoric and composition.

Many congratulations on your mid-century birthday.

Best regards and believe me,

Very truly yours,
HENRY O. FLIPPER

[On the morning of May 3, 1940, Henry Ossian Flipper's pen fell forever into an unaccustomed silence.]

NOTES

INTRODUCTION

1. J. Frank Dobie, *Apache Gold and Yaqui Silver* (Boston: Little, Brown, 1950), p. 203.

2. During the remainder of the nineteenth century the only other black graduates of West Point were John H. Alexander, class of 1887, and Charles Young, class of 1889. It was not until 1936 that Benjamin O. Davis, Jr., became the fourth black cadet to graduate.

3. Franklin M. Garrett, *Atlanta and Environs: A Chronicle of Its People and Events*, Vol. 1 (Athens: University of Georgia Press, 1954), pp. 511-512; and Henry O. Flipper, *The Colored Cadet at West Point: Autobiography of Lieut. Henry Ossian Flipper, U.S.A.; First Graduate Of Color From the U.S. Military Academy* (New York: H. Lee, 1878; rpt., New York: Arno Press, 1969), pp. 12-13.

4. Flipper, *Ibid.*, pp. 18-19.

5. Richard R. Wright, Jr., ed., *The Encyclopedia of the African Methodist Episcopal Church* (Alexandria, Virginia: Chadwyck-Healey, 1947), p. 104; and Carter G. Woodson, "Joseph Simeon Flipper," *The Journal of Negro History*, 30 (January, 1945), pp. 109-111.

6. Flipper, *The Colored Cadet at West Point*, pp. 18-19.

7. In 1866, immediately after the Civil War, Congress authorized four black Regular Army regiments. These units, the Ninth and Tenth Cavalry and the Twenty-fourth and Twenty-fifth Infantry, saw long combat service in the Indian Wars. With the exception of Flipper and two other black West Pointers who graduated during the 1880s, all the black units had white commissioned officers until 1901, three years after the Spanish-American War.

There are, at the least, four plausible explanations for the origin of the celebrated Indian sobriquet "Buffalo Soldiers" for the black Ninth and Tenth Cavalry

Regiments: 1.) The hair texture of most black troops reminded the Plains Indians of the woolly hair of the buffalo. Difficulty in grasping such hair is often cited as the reason why black troopers were rarely scalped in combat. 2.) The determination shown by black troopers in battle reminded the Indians of the fierceness of the cornered buffalo. 3.) The appellation was laudatory because the buffalo was a sacred animal in Plains Indian culture. This connection made it "bad medicine" to scalp a black trooper. 4.) The Indians coined the term from the buffalo robe overcoats worn by black cavalrymen during winter campaigns.

The Tenth Cavalry proudly adopted a buffalo head insignia and created a regimental song featuring a buffalo soldier theme.

8. For a biography of this controversial officer, see Paul H. Carlson, *"Pecos Bill:"* A *Military Biography of William R. Shafter* (College Station: Texas A&M University Press, 1989). See also, Robert M. Utley, "'Pecos Bill' on the Texas Frontier," *The American West*, 6 (January, 1969), pp. 4-13, 61-62.

9. The definitive biography of Greene is C. L. Sonnichsen, *Colonel Greene and the Copper Skyrocket* (Tucson: University of Arizona Press, 1974).

10. H.O. Flipper, report in possession of C.R. Ruggles, quoted in Dobie, *Apache Gold and Yaqui Silver*, pp. 204, 206. Flipper describes his first encounter with the Tayopa legend in 1889 at Hermosillo, Mexico, in *Apache Gold and Yaqui Silver*, pp. 204-205. Steve Wilson states that Flipper went to Spain in May, 1911. See "A Black Lieutenant in the Ranks," *American History Illustrated*, 17 (December, 1981), p. 37. James C. Cage and James M. Day write that Flipper did research at the Archivo General de las Indias in Sevilla and also mention the Hearst involvement. See *The Court Martial of Henry Ossian Flipper: West Point's First Black Graduate.* (El Paso: El Paso Corral of the Westerners, 1981), p. 31.

11. Letter from Fall, September 9, 1922, Washington, D.C., to Senator James W. Wadsworth, Jr. U. S. Department of the Interior (USDI) Records, Washington, D. C.

12. For an excellent study of Fall's career in the Southwest, an important aspect of his life often neglected by writers in favor of his later involvement in the Teapot Dome affair, see C.L. Sonnichsen, *Tularosa: Last of the Frontier West* (New York: Devin-Adair, 1960).

13. Sonnichsen, *Colonel Green and the Copper Skyrocket*, p. 221.

14. Letter, Fall to Wadsworth, USDI.

15. See letter from Flipper, February 25, 1913, El Paso, Texas, to Senator Albert B. Fall, Washington, D. C., Albert B. Fall Papers, Henry B. Huntington Library. San

Marino, California. (Hereinafter cited as A.B. Fall Papers.)

16. Jane Eppinga, "Henry O. Flipper in the Court of Private Land Claims: The Arizona Career of West Point's First Black Graduate," *The Journal of Arizona History*, 36 (Spring, 1995), p. 49.

17. Letter from Flipper, March 10, 1939, Atlanta, Georgia, to Joseph L. Martin, New York, New York, H.O. Flipper Collection, United States Military Academy Archives, West Point, New York.

18. Letter from Flipper, December 12, 1898, Santa Fe, New Mexico, to Booker T. Washington, Tuskegee, Alabama, in Louis R. Harlan, ed., *The Booker T. Washington Papers*, Vol. 4 (Champaign: University of Illinois Press, 1975), p. 529.

19. Letter from Fall, September 9, 1922, Washington, D.C., to Secretary of War John W. Weeks, USDI Records, Washington, D.C.

20. Letter from Fall to Wadsworth, USDI.

1—THE WESTERN MEMOIRS

1. Theodore D. Harris, Interview with Mrs. S. L. Flipper, Henry O. Flipper's sister-in-law (Atlanta, Georgia, July 12, 1960).

2. On January 1, 1878, at Fort Sill, Indian Territory (now Oklahoma).

3. A total eclipse of the sun was visible from the Wichita Indian Agency on July 29, 1879. Samuel Alfred Mitchell, *Eclipses of the Sun* (New York: Greenwood Press, 1957), p. 112.

4. Ben Clark was one of the frontier Army's most valued civilian scouts and Indian-language interpreters. He had distinguished himself on George Armstrong Custer's Washita expedition in 1868. During his career he also served as scout and interpreter under Generals Sully, Sheridan, Miles and Crook. He became an authority on the ethnology and customs of the Cheyenne and Arapahoe people. See Dan L. Thrapp, *Encyclopedia of Frontier Biography*, Vol. 1 (Spokane: Arthur H. Clark Company, 1990), pp. 274-275.

5. Captain Nicholas Nolan, commander of Flipper's Troop "A" of the Tenth Cavalry, was a respected field commander in Indian warfare operations. He befriended Flipper and sympathized with his ethnic problem because of his own feelings as a member of an Irish minority.

6. Annie and Mollie Dwyer were the daughters of Judge Thomas A. Dwyer, a prominent citizen of San Antonio, Texas. He was a former Army associate of Nicholas

Nolan. Mollie Dwyer's subsequent social contacts with Flipper were the cause of malicious gossip at Fort Sill and later at Forts Elliott and Davis in Texas.

7. "Mr. Lo" was a term often used in the nineteenth-century West to refer to the Plains Indians. It was derived from a line in Alexander Pope's *An Essay on Man* (1774): "Lo, the poor Indian!"

8. Whitall, born in Michigan, had an unusual military background. He was a midshipman at the Naval Academy when the Civil War broke out. He resigned from Annapolis and gained a commission as a Volunteer officer in the Union Army. After the war he was appointed an infantry officer in the Regular Army. Francis B. Heitman, *Historical Register and Dictionary of the United States Army: From Its Organization, September 29, 1789, to March 2, 1903*, Vol. 1 (Urbana: University of Illinois Press, 1965), p. 1026.

9. For a biography of this distinguished but lesser-known frontier officer see Homer K. Davidson, *Black Jack Davidson: A Cavalry Commander on the Western Frontier; The Life of General John W. Davidson* (Glendale, California: Arthur H. Clark Company, 1974). John J. Pershing did not hold a monopoly on the nickname "Black Jack" among white officers who served with black troops.

10. For more information about this remarkable individual who combined careers as Army officer and pioneer leader in American Indian education see Elaine Goodale Eastman, *Pratt: The Red Man's Moses* (Norman: University of Oklahoma Press, 1935); and Richard H. Pratt, *Battlefield and Classroom: Four Decades With the American Indian, 1864-1904*. Robert M. Utley, ed. (New Haven: Yale University Western Americana Series, Vol. 6, 1964). Pratt's Carlisle Indian School, founded in 1879, was the first and most influential institution devoted to American Indian education. It emphasized a white American academic and vocational curriculum. By 1912 Carlisle had become a major football power, producing the internationally famous Indian athlete Jim Thorpe.

11. In 1977, the drainage channel was commemorated as a National Historic Landmark.

12. Flipper refers to Wallace Tear. A native of Ohio, Tear enlisted in the Union Army, won a Volunteer commission and served with black troops. After the Civil War he received a Regular Army commission. He regiment, the Twenty-fourth Infantry, was a black unit with white officers. Tear resigned from the Army as a first lieutenant in 1883. See Heitman, *Historical Register*, p. 950.

13. Mills was actually a native of Indiana. The Mills Building, to which Flipper refers, is still a landmark in downtown El Paso. Begun in 1912 and completed in 1915, Anson Mills' name is commemorated in concrete above the entrance. It is one of

America's tallest pure masonry structures. Mills proudly described it as ". . . A monolithic cement building twelve stories high, containing no steel beams. . . . Said to be the first building of the kind erected in the United States." Anson Mills, *My Story* (Washington, D.C.: Press of Byron S. Adams, 1918), p. 245.

Anson Mills' career was closely associated with West Texas. After two years a cadet at West Point, he was found deficient in mathematics and, resigning, went to Texas. A pioneer resident of El Paso, he laid out the first plat of the city and in 1859, when sentiment favored changing the name from Franklin, proposed El Paso. As district surveyor for the State of Texas, he surveyed much of the Trans-Pecos country, including the military reservation of Fort Davis. At the outbreak of the Civil War Mills secured a commission in the Eighteenth Infantry and ended the war a captain with a brevet of lieutenant colonel. He fought in every battle in which the regiment engaged from 1861 to 1865. As a captain of the Third Cavalry, he played a notable part in the Sioux War of 1876-1877 and came to Fort Davis as major of the Tenth Cavalry, a rank he held, under Colonel Grierson, from 1878 to 1890. Promoted to colonel of the Third Cavalry in 1892, Mills retired a brigadier general in 1897 and served for the next twenty years as a member of the Mexican-American boundary commission. He invented the Mills woven military cartridge belt which became standard equipment in the U.S. Army and in most European armies as well; the basic pattern is still in use. He died in 1924. Robert M. Utley, *Fort Davis: National Historical Site, Texas* (Washington D. C.: National Park Service Handbook Series, No. 38, 1965), p. 61, n. 14.

14. Ward, from Pennsylvania, had graduated from West Point in 1871. His seventeen years of frontier service were marred by progressive alcoholism, a major problem among all ranks in the frontier Army. He was finally dismissed from the Army in 1888 primarily for chronic drunkenness.

15. Colladay, from Pennsylvania, followed a career pattern typical of many of the officers in the post-Civil War frontier Army. He enlisted in the Union Army and rose from the ranks to earn a Volunteer commission. At the end of the war he returned to civilian life but two years later, in 1867, he was able to qualify for a Regular Army commission as a second lieutenant. Heitman, *Historical Register*, p. 317.

16. Phillip L. Lee was born and raised in Virginia. He was, as Flipper states, related to General Robert E. Lee. Despite this heritage, he enlisted in a New York cavalry regiment in 1862 and rose to the rank of Volunteer second lieutenant by the war's end. After the war he won a Regular Army commission as a first lieutenant in 1866. In that same year he was one of the officers originally chosen for assignment to the newly authorized black Tenth Cavalry Regiment. Thus the ironical

nature of the military career of Robert E. Lee's cousin continued on the Southwestern frontier after the Civil War. *Ibid.*, p. 625.

17. Tascosa, Texas, had a reputation as one of the most lawless cattle towns in the West. See *The New Handbook of Texas*, Vol. 6 (Austin: Texas State Historical Association, 1996), p. 209.

18. Lawton was one of the Army's more colorful figures. Born in Ohio, he enlisted in an Indiana regiment of the Union Army. He won the Medal of Honor for heroism and rose to Colonel of Volunteers. As was common with Volunteer officers after the war, he accepted a drastic reduction in rank to obtain a Regular Army commission and was appointed a second lieutenant in 1866. In 1886 he led a special detachment that tracked down and captured Geronimo in Arizona. In the Spanish-American War he became a Volunteer major general. He was killed in action during the Philippine Insurrection in 1899. Fort Lawton, Washington, the prominent port of embarkation for the Pacific theater in World War II and the Korean War, was named for him. The near casualty of Lawton's wrath, Ralph Harrison, was from Missouri and had graduated from West Point in 1889. He served in the Spanish-American War and retired as a colonel in 1926. Heitman, *Historical Register*, p. 505; and George W. Cullum, *Register of Graduates and Former Cadets of the United States Military Academy: 1802-1980* (West Point, New York: Association of Graduates, U.S.M.A., 1980); p. 276.

19. Hatch, a New Yorker, had graduated from West Point in 1845. He served with distinction in the Mexican War. During the Civil War he won a Medal of Honor and became a Major General of Volunteers. After the war he reverted to a lower Regular Army rank as was the case with most officers. Heitman, *Historical Register*, p. 511; and Cullum, *Register of Graduates*, p. 238.

20. James A. Swift, from Maryland, served as an enlisted man in the post-Civil War Army and won a commission in 1878 in the Signal Corps. He transferred to the Cavalry in 1891, and served for a time in the black Ninth Cavalry Regiment. Heitman, *Historical Register*, p. 941.

21. Mrs. Maney's husband, Lieutenant James A. Maney, was born in Tennessee and was one of Flipper's West Point classmates. He served on the frontier throughout the Indian Wars, in Cuba during the Spanish-American War, in the China Relief Expedition, in the Philippine Insurrection, and retired as a colonel in 1911. Heitman, *Ibid.*, p. 687; and Cullum, *Register of Graduates*, p. 266.

22. Napoleon Bonaparte McLaughlin worked his way up from private to sergeant in the old Second Dragoons between 1850 and 1860 and was commissioned a second lieutenant when the Civil War broke out. He emerged from the war the colonel of a Massachusetts volunteer regiment and with a brevet of brigadier gen-

eral. He retired a major of the Tenth Cavalry in 1882, shortly after leaving Fort Davis, and died in 1887. Utley, *Fort Davis*, p. 61.

23. Commanding Officer of the Tenth Calvary Regiment, Benjamin H. Grierson, had won fame in the Civil War as a Union cavalry leader. When Flipper's troubles arose, he attempted unsuccessfully to have the charges reduced to avoid a General Court-Martial. During the trial he submitted a letter attesting to Flipper's honesty and good character and praised his devotion to duty and his military competence. After the verdict he tried unsuccessfully to persuade reviewing authorities to reduce Flipper's sentence of dismissal from the Army. Flipper refers to Colonel Grierson as General Grierson because it was customary in the post-Civil War Army to refer to officers by their higher temporary wartime rank if applicable. Grierson had risen to brevet major general during the Civil War. For an insightful biography of Grierson see William H. Leckie and Shirley A. Leckie, *Unlikely Warrior: General Benjamin Grierson and His Family* (Norman: University of Oklahoma Press, 1984). A scholarly account of Grierson's post-Civil War military career is Bruce J. Dinges, "Benjamin Grierson," in Paul Andrew Hutton, ed., *Soldiers West: Biographies From the Military Frontier* (Lincoln: University of Nebraska Press, 1985), pp. 157-176.

24. This attack occurred on October 14, 1880. Victorio, the Apache leader, was numbered among the dead.

25. Cooper had enlisted in the Union Army as a private in 1862. He gained his first experience commanding black troops during the Civil War when he was commissioned a second lieutenant in 1864. Heitman, *Historical Register*, p. 325. Cooper's daughter was the novelist Forestine Cooper Hooker.

26. Throughout his military career, Nordstrom was embroiled in numerous episodes of gross misconduct including a public physical assault with a club on one of his black sergeants. Flipper's harsh characterization of Nordstrom is supported by the latter's record.

27. Fifty-five years after this social visit at an isolated frontier Army post, Flipper recalled the elegant young South Carolinian arriving resplendent "in civilian clothes, top hat, Prince Albert coat, striped trousers and gloves." Letter from Flipper to Dr. Thomas Jefferson Flanagan, Atlanta, Georgia, July 6, 1936, in possession of editor.

28. In addition to accusing Wilhelmi of spying, Flipper later claimed that he conspired to drive him from the Army, and was guilty, with Lieutenant Charles Nordstrom, of stealing commissary funds from Flipper's quarters. Wilhelmi was a Prussian immigrant who had been medically discharged as a West Point cadet in 1873 for extreme nervous disorders. He received a direct commission as a second lieutenant in 1875 and was promoted to first lieutenant in 1880. He suffered from

nervous disorders throughout his Army career and they caused his death while still on active duty in 1886.

29. Flipper's court-martial trial convened at Fort Davis, Texas, on September 19, 1881, and concluded on December 7, 1881.

30. For a discussion of Flipper's court-martial see this book's "Introduction."

31. On arrival in El Paso, the only employment Flipper, as a black man with a court-martial conviction, could obtain was as manager of a steam laundry. *San Antonio Daily Express*, November 23, 1883, p. 1.

32. The Governor of Chihuahua was General Carlos Pacheco.

33. The Mexican Revolution, which had begun in 1910, was still raging in 1916.

34. S. H. Newman was the editor and publisher of the El Paso *Lone Star*.

35. Wood and Lawton were serving in the final campaign against the Apaches that culminated in the capture of Geronimo in 1886. Wood later commanded Theodore Roosevelt's celebrated Rough Riders in the Spanish-American War, became Military Governor of Cuba, was appointed Army Chief of Staff in 1910, and nearly won the Republican Presidential nomination in 1920.

36. Zebina N. Streeter led a bizarre career of crime on the Southwest frontier and in northern Mexico. He was eventually shot to death in Mexico in 1889. For an interesting account of his violent life see Thrapp, *Encyclopedia of Frontier Biography*, Vol. 3, pp. 1378-1379.

37. For a study of Flipper's role in the Nogales case and his activities in other Arizona land claim cases as Special Agent of the Department of Justice see Eppinga, "Henry O. Flipper in the Court of Private Land Claims," pp. 33-54.

38. For information about Jesse Grant's adventuresome life see William S. McFeely, *Grant: A Biography* (New York: W.W. Norton, 1981).

39. Flipper's successful candidate in his frontier-style political sculduggery against D. D. Altschul was James J. Chatham. He was the editor and publisher of the Nogales *Sunday Herald*, the Postmaster of Nogales, and soon to be a member of the Arizona Territorial legislature. Eppinga, "Henry O. Flipper in the Court of Private Land Claims," p. 34.

40. Robert D. Read, Jr. , from Tennessee, graduated from West Point fifty-sixth in a class of seventy-six in 1877. Flipper, despite the pressures of social ostracism, graduated six places higher, fiftieth, in the same class. After an unexceptional Army career, Read retired as a colonel in 1914. Heitman, *Historical Register*, p. 819, and Cullum, *Register of Graduates*, p. 266.

41. When James J. Chatham turned his newspaper over to Flipper during the spring of 1895, Flipper became the first black editor of a white-owned newspaper in Arizona history. Eppinga, "Henry O. Flipper in the Court of Private Land Claims," p. 50. The following year, Flipper also promoted his 1896 appointment as a U.S. Deputy Mineral inspector by placing this notice in the November 21, 1896, Nogales *Oasis* (Eppinga, *Ibid.*, pp. 50-51):

HENRY O. FLIPPER
U.S. DEPUTY MINERAL SURVEYOR
Mine and Land Surveys
United States or Mexico
Thorough Acquaintance with
Mexican Land and Mining Laws
Translations in English and
Spanish. Notary Public.
NOGALES, ARIZONA

42. Charles R. Ward died in New York City in 1901. Cullum, *Register of Graduates*, p. 261.

43. Dr. Edward R. Perrin, like John Tyler Morgan, was also a native of Alabama and had also served in the Confederate Army during the Civil War. Eppinga, "Henry O. Flipper in the Court of Private Land Claims," p. 46.

44. Morgan had been a lawyer before the Civil War. He became a brigadier general in the Confederate army and reentered politics after the war. In the Senate he was an advocate of white supremacy.

45. The Camerons, father and son, were wealthy financiers who dominated the Republican Party in Pennsylvania during the late nineteenth century.

46. For more details of the Perrin case see Eppinga, "Henry O. Flipper in the Court of Private Land Claims," p. 46-47.

47. Richard Olney, the attorney general, was an expansionist soon to play a key role in the 1895 dispute with Great Britain over Venezuela while serving as Grover Cleveland's Secretary of State.

48. The U.S. attorney who gave this testimonial to Flipper's professional competence and good character was U.S. Prosecutor Matthew G. Reynolds. He had earlier attended the United States Naval Academy at Annapolis. Eppinga, "Henry O. Flipper in the Court of Private Land Claims," pp. 36 and 38.

49. Charles Alexander was a Tuskegee Institute faculty member. Tuskegee Institute, a college for black students, was founded in Alabama in 1881. Booker T. Washington was president from its founding until his death in 1915. The school

personified Washington's philosophy of vocational education for black college students. During World War II, America's first black fighter pilots were trained at Tuskegee Institute, including future Air Force Lieutenant General Benjamin O. Davis, Jr. He was the fourth black graduate of West Point, class of 1936, and the first to graduate in the twentieth century.

50. Judson W. Lyons was a black attorney from Georgia and one of the few black members of the Republican National Committee. The position of Register of the Treasury had become one of the federal appointments customarily reserved for blacks whenever the Republicans controlled the administration.

51. William S. Scarborough, a black scholar of linguistics, later became president of Wilberforce University. Located in Wilberforce, Ohio, the school was one of a few black colleges functioning in a northern state. During this period it held a prominent place among black American educational institutions.

52. "Fighting Joe" Wheeler had the extraordinary distinction of combat command as a Confederate lieutenant general during the Civil War and later as a major general in the United States Army during the Spanish-American War. He also served over sixteen years in Congress after the Civil War and rose to chair the powerful House Ways and Means Committee. By the turn of the century, Wheeler had become a national symbol of sectional reconciliation.

53. McKay had served from 1881 to 1897 until denied reenlistment in the latter year. He was seeking reinstatement in the Army himself when he met Flipper. McKay persuaded Wisconsin Congressman Michael Griffin to introduce the first bill authorizing a review of Flipper's court-martial. Steve Wilson, "A Black Lieutenant in the Ranks," pp. 30-39.

54. Charles Young, of Ohio, was the third black graduate of West Point, class of 1889. He had a twenty-nine year military career and rose to the rank of colonel.

55. In 1916, a punitive expedition under Brigadier General John J. Pershing invaded Northern Mexico in response to a raid on Columbus, New Mexico, by General Pancho Villa's revolutionary forces.

56. Benjamin O. Davis, Sr., who did not attend West Point, became the Army's first black brigadier general in 1940. His son, Benjamin O. Davis, Jr., was the fourth black graduate of West Point, class of 1936. He rose to the rank of lieutenant general in the United States Air Force.

57. Before racial integration of the Army after World War II, it was standard policy to assign the Army's few black officers to Reserve Officers Training Corps duty at black colleges whenever feasible. The purpose was to avoid potential racial friction within the Regular Army.

58. P.B.S. Pinchback had been a black lieutenant governor of Louisiana during Reconstruction. Robert H. Terrell, Judge of the Municipal Court of Washington, D. C., was the leading black jurist of his era.

59. Barber, from Vermont, graduated from Williams College in 1857. He studied law under future President Chester Alan Arthur and was admitted to the bar in 1859. He enlisted in the Union Army and rose to Volunteer major. He received a Regular Army commission after the war. Capitalizing on his administrative ability, Barber served most of his career in the Adjutant-General's Department. Before retirement in 1901, he had served in the Spanish-American War as a Volunteer brigadier general.

60. Clous, a German immigrant, enlisted in the Army in 1857 and won a Regular Army commission during the Civil War. After the war he specialized in military law. He was appointed to the judge-advocate (legal) corps and built a reputation as a relentless prosecutor in court-martial trials. Although his aggressive legal tactics made him unpopular with many brother officers, he became judge-advocate general of the Army in 1901.

61. Mrs. Terrell was the nation's most prominent female black leader.

62. By 1898, Mrs. Dunbar's husband had become America's most celebrated black poet.

63. In 1914, McAdoo had become President Woodrow Wilson's son-in-law.

64. For more information about Greene and Fall see the editor's "Introduction."

65. General Frisbie's interest in helping Flipper utilize his military knowledge may have stemmed from Frisbie's experiences while commanding a black cavalry regiment in the Union Army during the Civil War. A New Yorker, Frisbie rose to Volunteer brigadier general. Heitman, *Historical Register*, p. 438. After the war he returned to his civilian profession of engineering.

2—ARMY AND CIVILIAN LETTERS

1. Letter from Flipper, January 4, 1878, Fort Sill, Indian Territory [Oklahoma], to Albert Todd, comp., *The Class of '77 at the United States Military Academy* (Cambridge, Massachusetts: Riverside Press, 1878), p. 44.

2. Officer of the Day, Post Guard Reports, Fort Sill, I. T., August 28, 1878. Fort Sill, Oklahoma, Museum.

3. Letter from Flipper, March 29, 1879, Fort Elliott, Texas, newspaper clipping, S. E. Tillman Scrapbook. United States Military Academy Library Archives. West Point, New York.

4. *Ibid.*

5. Edmunds, from Michigan, graduated from West Point in 1871. He served in the Nez Percé campaign in 1877 and in Cuba during the Spanish-American War. He died of yellow fever in Cuba in 1900 at the rank of major. At Fort Davis in 1881 he was a first lieutenant in Colonel Shafter's First Infantry Regiment. He became commissary officer when Shafter removed Flipper from that post. Edmunds was one of the officers who searched Flipper's quarters and impounded his papers and personal effects. Heitman, *Historical Register*, p. 397; and Cullum, *Register of Graduates*, p. 260.

6. Small was a major in 1881 rather than a colonel. A native of Pennsylvania, he graduated from West Point in 1855. Most of his Army career was spent as a commissary specialist. He distinguished himself in that capacity during the Civil War and rose to brevet brigadier general. In 1889, as a lieutenant colonel, he was appointed the Army's acting commissary general. During Flipper's troubles, Small was serving as chief commissary officer for the Department of Texas. Heitman, *Historical Register*, p. 892; and Cullum, *Register of Graduates*, p. 247.

7. Chamberlain was a watchmaker in the nearby town of Fort Davis, Texas, and one of Flipper's white civilian friends. He testified as a witness for the defense at Flipper's trial.

8. Record of the Court-Martial of Second Lieutenant Henry O. Flipper, pp. 503-506, National Archives and Records Administration, Washington D.C.

9. Letter from Flipper, November 15, 1883, El Paso, Texas, to F. W. May, El Paso, Texas. Original appeared in the *San Antonio Daily Express*, November 23, 1883, p. 1. The editor thanks Dr. Bruce J. Dinges, editor of *The Journal of Arizona History*, whose research discovered this article, for sharing it with him. For studies of Flipper's court-martial trial, see Dinges, "The Court-Martial of Lt. Henry O. Flipper," *The American West*, Vol. 9 (January, 1972), pp. 12-17, 59-61; and Charles M. Robinson, III, *The Court-Martial of Lieutenant Henry Flipper* (El Paso: Texas Western Press, 1994).

10. El Paso, Texas, *Lone Star*, February 9, 1884, p. 1.

11. Alger, from Michigan, was a Civil War veteran who had entered Republican politics after the war. During the war he had risen to Volunteer major general. He served as President William McKinley's secretary of war from 1897 to 1899. He was widely criticized for America's lack of preparedness and military inefficiency in the early stage of the Spanish-American War.

12. The telegram is quoted from "Petition for Restoral to the Service: Statement and Brief of Petitioner in the Matter of the Court-Martial of Henry Ossian Flipper,

Second Lieutenant, Tenth Cavalry, U. S. Army." U.S. Congress, House Committee on Military Affairs, Fifty-fifth Congress, Second Session, 1899, pp. 58-59.

3—TWO BLACK FRONTIERSMEN: HENRY FLIPPER AND ESTEVANICO

1. W. E. B. Du Bois, *The Gift of Black Folk* (Boston, 1924; rpt., Hackensack, New Jersy: Kraus International Publishers, 1975), p. 43, n. 15.

2. Vol. 13, pp. 2-21.

3. An influential black educator who later had a successful business career as a pioneering black banker. During the Spanish-American War, he served as an army paymaster with the rank of major.

4. Flipper had attended the American Missionary Society's newly founded Atlanta University for black students before entering West Point in 1873.

5. Bandelier's anthropological and historical research as early as 1880 to 1889 in the Southwest helped build the foundation for modern scientific scholarship on that region. Bandelier National Monument near Santa Fe, New Mexico, is named for him.

4—LEGEND OF THE BLACK ROBIN HOOD OF THE BORDERLANDS: HENRY FLIPPER AND PANCHO VILLA

1. Theodore D. Harris, interview with R. L. Andrews (El Paso, Texas, March 5, 1961). Mr. Andrews served as an aviator for Pancho Villa and knew him personally. He still attests to Villa's negroid features and to the prevalence of the Caribbean African ancestry rumor during those years.

2. Theodore D. Harris, interview with Haldeen Braddy (El Paso, Texas, March 4, 1961).

3. Edward B. Reuter, *The Mulatto in the United States* (Boston, 1918; rpt., Westport, Connecticut: Greenwood Press, 1969), p. 248, n. 8.

4. H. H. Dunn, *The Crimson Jester: Zapata of Mexico* (New York, 1933; rpt., New York: Gordon Press, 1976), pp. 166, 232, 236-241.

5. Copy in A. B. Fall Papers, Washington, D.C.

6. Letter from Flipper, August 14, 1914, El Paso, Texas, to Fall, Washington, D.C., Fall Papers.

7. Theodore D. Harris, interview with Mrs. S. L. Flipper (Atlanta, Georgia, July 12, 1960).

8. In 1906, three companies of Regular Army black soldiers from the Twenty-fifth Infantry were dishonorably discharged for alleged participation in a race riot at Brownsville, Texas.

9. In a nationally publicized incident in 1880, Whittaker, a black cadet at West Point, accused several white cadets of mutilating him. A board of investigation concluded that the wounds were self-inflicted in a desperate attempt by Whittaker to avoid the disciplinary consequences of academic deficiencies.

10. Frederick Funston's career was an exciting saga. Raised in Kansas, he received a commission in the Cuban rebel army in 1896 and fought against the Spaniards. He became a Volunteer colonel in the U.S. Army in the Spanish-American War, won a Medal of Honor in the Philippine Insurrection, and captured the rebel leader Emilio Aguinaldo in a daring raid. His reward was a transfer from Volunteer brigadier general to Regular Army brigadier general. He led Army relief efforts after the 1906 San Francisco earthquake and commanded the American occupation forces at Veracruz, Mexico, in 1914. Promoted to major general, he exercised, from San Antonio, Texas, overall responsibility for Brigadier General John J. Pershing's 1916 punitive expedition against Pancho Villa in Mexico. Funston died at age fifty-one in 1917. Robert McHenry, ed., *Webster's American Military Biographies* (Springfield, Massachusetts: G. and C. Merriam, 1978) pp. 132-133. Funston's death, on the eve of America's entry into World War I, was deemed a major loss to the Army's leadership. He would have been one of the leading candidates to command the American Expeditionary Force in France, a post eventually given to Pershing, Frederick Funston's immediate subordinate on the Mexican border. Frank E. Vandiver. *Black Jack: The Life and Times of John J. Pershing*, Vol. 2 (College Station: Texas A&M University Press, 1977), p. 671-672.

5—THE PATH TO CAPITOL HILL

1. Sonnichsen, *Colonel Greene and the Copper Skyrocket*, p. 230.

2. Letter from Flipper, February 25, 1914, El Paso, Texas, to Fall, Washington, D.C., Fall Papers.

3. Letter from Fall, August 10, 1914, Washington, D.C., to Flipper, El Paso, Texas, Fall Papers.

4. Letter from Flipper, August 15, 1914, El Paso, Texas, to Fall, Washington, D.C., Fall Papers.

5. Felix Diaz was the nephew of deposed dictator Porfirio Diaz. He led unsuccessful counter-revolts for the purpose of restoring the old order in Mexico.

6. General Alvaro Obregón was initially allied with Villa but became one of his most formidable opponents as the Mexican Revolution progressed. By the end of the Revolution in 1920, Obreg n emerged as President of Mexico.

7. Letter from Flipper, October 9, 1914, El Paso, Texas, to Fall, Washington, D.C., Fall Papers.

8. Letter from Flipper, January 9, 1916, El Paso, Texas, to Fall, Washington, D.C. [Subject: Harrison Rather], Fall Papers.

9. Flipper is referring to the Presidio of San Francisco in California.

10. Letter from Flipper, January 9, 1916, El Paso, Texas, to Fall, Washington, D.C. [Subject: Army Reform], Fall Papers.

11. Letter from Sergt. B. M. McKay, August 12, 1919, Washington, D.C., to Fall, Washington, D.C., Fall Papers.

12. Telegram from Fall, August 26, 1919, Washington, D.C., to Flipper, El Paso, Texas, Fall Papers.

13. Letter from Dan M. Jackson, August 27, Washington, D.C. , to McKay, Washington, D.C., Fall Papers.

14. Telegram from Flipper, August 27, 1919, El Paso, Texas, to Fall, Washington, D. C., Fall Papers.

15. Telegram from Fall, August 28, 1919, Washington, D.C., to Flipper, El Paso, Texas, Fall Papers.

16. Harrison Walthall was an El Paso attorney and a prominent member of the city's business community.

17. Letter from Flipper, August 29, 1919, El Paso, Texas, to Fall, Washington, D.C., Fall Papers.

18. Telegram from Fall, September 2, 1919, Washington, D.C., to Flipper, El Paso, Texas, Fall Papers.

19. Telegram from Flipper, September 10, 1919, El Paso, Texas, to Fall, Washington, D.C., Fall Papers.

20. Telegram from Fall, September 11, 1919, Washington, D.C., to Flipper, El Paso, Texas, Fall Papers.

21. Telegram from Flipper, September 15, 1919, El Paso, Texas, to Fall, Washington, D.C., Fall Papers.

22. Letter to Theodore D. Harris from Robert A. Brenkworth, Financial Clerk, United States Senate. November 9, 1961.

23. Personnel folder of Henry O. Flipper, Department of the Interior, Federal Records Center, St. Louis, Missouri.

24. Buckley was the father of William F. Buckley, Jr., prominent conservative author, editor, and spokesman.

25. Wilson, "A Black Lieutenant in the Ranks," p. 38.

6—FLIPPER'S LATER RECOLLECTIONS

1. Letter from Flipper to Joseph L. Martin, New York, New York, H.O. Flipper Collection, United States Military Academy Archives, West Point, New York.

2. Theodore D. Harris, interview with Dr. Thomas Jefferson Flanagan (Atlanta, Georgia, July 15, 1960). The editor conducted several interviews with Dr. Flanagan during July, 1960, in Atlanta.

3. Smith was nicknamed "Cotton Ed" because of his vigorous political support of cotton and other agricultural interests. He was also an unwavering advocate of white supremacy in the South.

4. Mitchell was a black Democratic congressman from Chicago.

5. Their years of graduation were: Flipper, 1877; Alexander, 1887; Young, 1889; and Davis, Jr., 1936.

6. Talmadge became a senator from Georgia after serving as governor. He was an outspoken white supremacist. His son, Herman Talmadge, was later to become a prominent senator from Georgia. Both were conservative Democrats.

7. Farley, nicknamed "Genial Jim," managed Franklin Roosevelt's 1932 and 1936 presidential campaigns. He became chairman of the Democratic National Committee and was named postmaster general by President Roosevelt. In that capacity he dispensed the New Deal's political patronage appointments. In 1940 Farley split bitterly with Roosevelt over the latter's determination to seek an unprecedented third term.

8. Lily-white was a common negative term in the 1930s denoting an individual or a policy that advocated strict racial segregation.

9. All letters from Flipper to Flanagan quoted are in the possession of the editor.

10. Letter from Flipper, February 16, 1931, Washington, D.C., to Roberto Pardo, Caracas, Venezuela, United States Military Academy Archives, West Point, New York.

11. The first black midshipman to graduate from the Naval Academy at Annapolis, Wesley A. Brown, did so in 1949.

12. A method of protest by striking labor-union members that was in fashion during the Great Depression of the 1930s.

13. The National Association for the Advancement of Colored People was founded in 1909. One of its principle organizers was the militant W.E.B. Du Bois. Through the 1930s it specialized in judicial cases defending civil rights and in lobbying for civil rights legislation.

14. In 1944 (four years after Flipper's death), following several years of litigation, the U.S. Supreme Court finally ruled in *Smith v. Allwright* that white primary elections were unconstitutional. The Court held that such racially exclusive elections violated provisions of the fifteenth amendment of the constitution.

15. Kelly Miller was a mathematics professor and dean at Howard University in Washington, D.C. In the controversy that developed over opposing philosophies for black advancement between the gradualist Booker T. Washington and the militant W.E.B. Du Bois, Miller became known for expressing a middle-ground position. Howard University, a Federally supported institution, vied with the private Atlanta University as America's leading center for black higher education.

16. Flipper refers to Hugo LaFayette Black of Alabama. Appointed to the Supreme Court by Roosevelt in 1937, Black admitted to having joined the Ku Klux Klan in the mid-1920s. He renounced Klan sympathies, however, and proved to be a liberal associate justice.

17. The military and District of Columbia voting restrictions that Flipper wrote of in 1937 have subsequently been eliminated.

18. This school was the black branch of Texas A&M College. It later became Prairie View A&M University.

19. This educator was Thomas S. Gathright, the first president of Texas A&M.

20. During the first decade of the twentieth century Alexander gained some prominence as a black journalist and editor on racial issues. He published *Alexander's Magazine* and espoused the views of Booker T. Washington, who subsidized some of Alexander's publications.

SUGGESTED READINGS

The following books and articles either deal with the life and career of Henry O. Flipper or contain informative material about him. The list is a guide for the interested reader but is not a complete bibliography of the subject.

BOOKS

Cage, James C. and Day, James M. *The Court Martial of Henry Ossian Flipper: West Point's First Black Graduate*. El Paso, Texas: El Paso Corral of the Westerners, 1981.

Carlson, Paul H. *"Pecos Bill": A Military Biography of William R. Shafter*. College Station: Texas A&M University Press, 1989.

Carroll, John M., ed. *The Black Military Experience in the American West*. New York: Liveright, 1971.

Dobie, J. Frank. *Apache Gold and Yaqui Silver*. Boston: Little, Brown, 1950.

Eppinga, Jane. *Henry Ossian Flipper: West Point's First Black Graduate*. Plano: Republic of Texas Press, 1996.

Flipper, Henry Ossian. *The Colored Cadet at West Point: Autobiography of Lieut. Henry Ossian Flipper, U.S.A., First Graduate of Color from the U.S. Military Academy*. New York: H. Lee, 1878; Rpt., New York: Arno Press, 1969.

Leckie, William H. *The Buffalo Soldiers: A Narrative of the Negro Cavalry in the West*. Norman: University of Oklahoma Press, 1967.

Leckie, William H. and Leckie, Shirley A. *Unlikely Warrior: General Benjamin Grierson and His Family*. Norman: University of Oklahoma Press, 1984.

Owen, Gordon R. *The Two Alberts: Fountain and Fall*. Las Cruces, New Mexico: Yucca Tree Press, 1997.

Robinson, Charles M., III. *The Court-Martial of Lieutenant Henry Flipper*. El Paso: Texas Western Press, 1994.

Sonnichsen, C.L. *Colonel Greene and the Copper Skyrocket*. Tucson: University of Arizona Press, 1974.

Thrapp, Dan L. *Encyclopedia of Frontier Biography*. 4 Volumes. Spokane, Washington: Arthur H. Clark Company, 1990-94.

ARTICLES

Brown, Wesley A. "Eleven Men of West Point," *The Negro History Bulletin*, 19 (April, 1956), pp. 146-157. This article is of additional interest because Brown was the first black graduate of the U.S. Naval Academy at Annapolis, class of 1949.

Dinges, Bruce J. "The Court-Martial of Lieutenant Henry O. Flipper," *The American West*, 9 (January, 1972), pp. 12-17; 59-61.

Eppinga, Jane. "Henry O. Flipper in the Court of Private Land Claims: The Arizona Career of West Point's First Black Graduate," *The Journal of Arizona History*, 36 (Spring, 1995), pp. 33-54.

Johnson, Barry C. "Flipper's Dismissal: The Ruin of Lt. Henry O. Flipper, U.S.A.—First Coloured Graduate of West Point," *The Silver Jubilee Publication of the English Westerners' Society*. London, 1980, pp. 133-226.

McClung, Donald R. "Second Lieutenant Henry O. Flipper: A Negro Officer on the West Texas Frontier," *West Texas Historical Association Year Book*, 47 (1971), Abilene, Texas, pp. 12-17; 56-61.

Warner, Ezra J., "A Black Man in the Long Gray Line," *American History Illustrated*, 4 (January, 1970), pp. 30-38.

Wilson, Steve. "A Black Lieutenant in the Ranks, "*American History Illustrated* 17 (December, 1983), pp. 30-39.

For additional biographical information about Army officers mentioned in this book, the following works are useful.

Altshuler, Constance W. *Cavalry Yellow and Infantry Blue: Army Officers in Arizona Between 1851 and 1886.* Tucson: Arizona Historical Society, 1991.

————. *Starting With Defiance: Nineteenth Century Arizona Military Posts.* Tucson: Arizona Historical Society, 1983.

Cullum, George W. *Register of Graduates and Former Cadets of the United States Military Academy.* West Point, New York: Association of Graduate, U.S.M.A. Published annually.

Heitman, Francis B. *Historical Register and Dictionary of the United States Army: From Its Organization, September 29, 1789, to March 2, 1903.* Two Volumes. Washington, D.C.: Government Printing Office, 1903; Rpt., Urbana: University of Illinois Press, 1965.

McHenry, Robert, ed. *Webster's American Military Biographies.* Springfield, Massachusetts: G. and C. Merriam, 1978.

For information about the history, state of preservation or restoration, and accessibility for visitors to the frontier Army posts mentioned in this book, the following works are useful.

Ferris, Robert G., ed. *Soldier and Brave: Historic Places Associated with Indian Affairs and the Indian Wars in the Trans-Mississippi West.* Washington, D.C.: National Park Service, 1971.

Frazer, Robert W. *Forts of the West: Military Forts and Presidios and Posts Commonly Called Forts West of the Mississippi River to 1898.* Norman: University of Oklahoma Press, 1977.

Haley, J. Evetts. *Fort Concho and the Texas Frontier*. San Angelo, Texas: San Angelo Standard Times, 1952.

Hart, Herbert M. *Old Forts of the Far West*. Seattle: Superior Publishing Company, 1965.

————. *Old Forts of the Southwest*. New York: Bonanza Books, 1964.

————. *Pioneer Forts of the West*. New York: Bonanza Books, 1967.

————. *Tour Guide to Old Western Forts: The Posts and Camps of the Army, Navy and Marines on the Western Frontier, 1804-1916*. Boulder, Colorado: Pruett Publishing Company, 1980.

Prucha, Francis P. *A Guide to the Military Posts of the United States, 1789-1895*. Madison, Wisconsin: State Historical Society of Wisconsin, 1964.

Ruth, Kent. *Great Day in the West: Forts, Posts, and Rendezvous Beyond the Mississippi*. Norman: University of Oklahoma Press, 1963.

Scobee, Barry. *Old Fort Davis*. San Antonio: Naylor Company, 1947

Utley, Robert M. *Fort Davis: National Historical Site, Texas*. Washington, D.C.: National Park Service Handbook Series, No. 38, 1965.

Wooster, Robert. *Fort Davis: Outpost on the Texas Frontier*. Austin: Texas State Historical Association, 1994.

Dwyer, Miss Mollie, 5, 18, 19, 30, 31, 37, 51, 161 n. 6
Dwyer, Judge Thomas A., 161 n. 6

Eagle Springs, Texas, 34, 35
Eclipse of the sun, 18, 161 n. 3
Economy: collapse of 1929, 12; inflation, 119; Great Depression 146-47, 175 n. 12
Edmunds, Lieutenant Frank H., 77, 170 n. 5
El Paso, Texas, 3, 7, 15, 25, 39, 44, 51, 94, 101-05, 116, 137, 163 n. 13,
El Paso Lone Star, 44, 81, 166 n. 34
Espejo, Antonio de, 92
Estavanico: 9, 83-92; Castaneda's charges against, 88; death at Cibola, 90; discovery of Arizona and New Mexico, 91; as interpreter, 87

Fall, Senator Albert Bacon: 13-15, 62, 95, 97, 99, 116-22; and William Greene, 10, 105; interests in Mexico, 11, 105-11; as Secretary of the Interior, 12, 122; as head of Senate investigating committee on Mexico, 11-12, 105-11; and Teapot Dome scandal, 10, 122.
Farley, James A. "Genial Jim," 129, 174 n. 7
Ferguson, Governor "Ma," 138
Fisk University, 86
Flanagan, Dr. Thomas Jefferson, 13, 125; Flipper's letters to, 125-58
Flipper, Henry Ossian: 2 , 74, 85, 127; Army active duty assignments, 4, 18, 19, 25, 27, 28, 31, 80-81, 150-51; Army field service assignments, 35; attempts to clear military record, 14-15, 56-59, 168 n. 53; attitudes toward African Americans, 130, 131, 141; attitudes toward Mexicans, 40, 43-44, 47-48, 81; black Army officers, views on role of, 149-52; childhood, 3-4; as civil engineer, see civil engineering and Flipper's Ditch; Constitution (U.S.), views on, 13, 126, 137-39, 144-45, 153, 155; court-martial 5-7, 54, 76-80 (statement to the Court), 166 n. 29; dismissal from Army, 6-7, 37, 39, 53, 166 n. 31; as editor 9, 51; erudition and attitudes toward education, 128, 130, 131, 132, 133, 135, 154, 156-57; financial difficulties, 12, 118-20; health of, 14, 35; as Indian fighter, 32-35; and international relations, 11, 105-06, 109-110; labor, views on, 133-34, 145-46; language use, accuracy of, 72, 126; as legal consultant and mining engineer, 10-12, 61-63, 103-105, 122, 125; Mexican Revolution, views on, 103; as "marginal man," 15, 142-43; as money manager, 5, 80; officer candidate plan, 113-14; patriotism of, 66, 81, 101; personal qualities, 7, 27, 31, 32, 52, 64, 72; as pioneer in professions, 5, 51, 81, 83, 167 n. 41; political views, 13, 97, 105, 125-26, 128, 130, 132-33, 135-38, 152-154; press, attitude to, 100, 156-57; publications of, see titles; race relations, views on, 13, 97, 126, 128-30, 150-51; relationships with women, 6, 13, 17; researches in Spain 10, 160 n. 10; as scholar of Spanish Southwest, 7, 9, 54, 83-92; sign language, knowledge of, 19; on slavery, 144-45; in South America, 12; Spanish, fluency in, 7, 9, 10-12 40, 52, 55, 83, 104, 119; Spanish land-grant law, knowledge of, 7, 52, 55, 103; as Special Agent of U.S. Justice

Department 9, 49, 51, 52, 55, 61, 81, 103; as Special Assistant to Secretary of Interior, 12, 122, and see Fall, Albert B.; states rights, views on, 13, 126, 128, 129, 133-37, 147, 153-55; as surveyor-mapmaker, 28, 39-40, 45-48, 55, 73, 103, and as U. S. Deputy Mineral Surveyor, 167 n. 41; and Tayopa mine, 9-10, 160 n. 10; and Teapot Dome scandal, 13; on Pancho Villa, 11-13, 93-104. See also Court of Private Land Claims, Democratic Party, Dwyer, Mollie, Republicans, Race relations, United States Attorney, United States Department of Justice.

Flipper, Reverend Joseph Simeon (brother), 3-4; 13, 125

Flipper, Mrs. S. L. (sister-in-law), 13, 98

Flipper's Ditch, 5, 22, 162 n. 11

Florida, and Estevanico, 88

Folklore, in Villa affair, 95-99. See also Tayopa.

Forrest, Nathan Bedford, 150

Fort Concho, Texas, 4, 5, 25

Fort Davis, Texas: 4, 5, 14, 32, 35-37, 42, 163 n. 13, 165 n. 22, 170 n. 5; court-martial tribunal at 6, 76-80

Fort Elliott, Texas, 4, 24, 27-31, 72

Fort Lawton, Washington, 164 n. 18

Fort Leavenworth, Kansas, 26

Fort Quitman, Texas, 4, 32

Fort Sill, Indian Territory, 4, 5, 17, 18, 20, 23, 25-29, 32, 36, 71-72. See also Flipper's Ditch.

Fort Stockton, Texas, 35, 42

Fort Supply, Indian Territory, 30

Fort Worth, Texas, 23-24, 28, 29

Freeman, J. C., 4

Fresno Spring, Texas, 34, 35

Frisbie, General H. N., 66, 169 n. 65

Fronteras, Mexico, 45

Funston, Major General Frederick, 102, 172 n. 10

Gainesville, Texas, 5, 27

Gallagher, Father_____, 65, 66

Galveston, Texas, 45

Gathright, Thomas S., 175 n. 19

Geronimo, 164 n. 18, 166 n. 35. See also Apache Indians.

Geyer, Representative Lee, 153, 155. See also poll tax.

Gibbons, Floyd, 93

Globe-Democrat, 66

Grant, General Ulysses S., 50

Grant, Jesse (son of Ulysses), 50

Greene, Colonel William (Bill) Cornell: 8, 10, 62, 64, 65; and Flipper, 10; and Gold-Silver Company, 109; and Hearst, 10; and Sierra Mining Company, 11, 105, 119

Grierson, General B. H.: 32-34, 33, 163 n. 13, attempts to reduce court-martial charges, 165 n. 23,

Griffin, Congressman Michael, 168 n. 53

Hampton, General Wade, 37

Hampton, Lieutenant Wade, 37, 165 n. 27

Harding, President Warren G.: administration, 10; and A. B. Fall, 12, 122

Harrison, General _____, 39

Harrison, Lieutenant Ralph, 30, 164 n. 18

Hatch, Lieutenant Colonel John W., 30, 164 n. 19

Hawikuh, 90, 91

Heidelberg University, 5. See also Flipper's Ditch.

Hennings, Congressman and Senator Thomas C., 130, 131

Hill, Mrs. _____ (neice of Jefferson Davis), 49

105, 166 n. 33, 173 n. 6; blacks in Mexican Army, 101-102; American troops in Mexico, 103, 172 n. 10; foreign relations during, 105; and mining operations during, 108-09. *See also* Villa, General Francisco.

Mexicans: 28; customs and social life, 40-42, 43-45, 66, 68; education of, 40; intermarriage, 47, 48; merchants, 41; religious feasts, 43; salt making, 41; as servants, 64; smuggling, 44; social life, 65. *See also* race relations.

Mexico: 32, 34; currency of 41; government survey concessions, 39; churches, 48; climate and terrain of 41-42; jails, 44; police in, 66; small towns, description of, 48. *See also* mining engineering, investors in; plants; Tayopa mine.

Mexico City, 65, 66, 86

Military Academy of Mexico, Chapultepec, 66, 102

Miller, Dean Kelly, 144, 156, 175 n. 15

Mills, Major Anson, 25, 162 n. 13

Mines Company of America, 108

Mining engineering: company store, 64; crews, 63; intercompany conflicts, 63; investors in, 62, 104;

Mitchell, Representative Arthur W., 128, 174 n. 4

Morgan, Senator J. T., 51, 52, 167 n. 44

Mulatto, 94. *See also* Reuter, Edward B.

NAACP, 136, 147, 148, 175 n. 13

Neutrality Act, 150

New Deal, 126, 128, 145, 146, 148, 174 n. 7

Newman, S. H., 166 n. 34

New Mexico, 32; Coronado's expedition into, 86

New Mexico Historical Review, 9

Newspapers and journals, see frontier, *El Paso Lone Star, Nogales Oasis, Nogales Sunday Herald, Old Santa Fe*; other, *African Methodist Episcopal Review, Alexander's Magazine, Atlanta Daily World, Boston Advertiser, The Call, Macon Telegraph, Washington Eagle, Washington Post, Globe-Democrat.*

Nez Percé Indians, 170 n. 5

Nixon, Dr. L. A., 137

Niza, Friar Marcos de, 9, 84, 89-92

Nogales, Arizona Territory: 13, 45, 49, 51-53, 94; city charter 7; constitutional convention, 49; as headquarters, surveying practice 7, 49; land-grant case, 49, 103; publication site, 9

Nogales Sunday Herald: Chatham, James J., as editor of, 7, 50; Flipper as editor of, 9, 51

Nogales Oasis, 167 n. 41

Nolan, Captain Nicholas, 5, 22, 24, 25, 27, 29, 32, 51

Nolan, Mrs. Annie (nee Dwyer), 19, 51

Nordstrom, Lieutenant Charles E., 37, 39, 51, 165 n. 26, 165 n. 28

Obregón, General Alvaro, 110, 173 n. 6

Ocampo, Mexico, 41, 45, 63, 105

Old Santa Fe, see *New Mexico Historical Review*

Olney, Richard, 103, 167 n. 47

Onorato, Friar _____, 88

Pacheco, General Carlos, 166 n. 32

Pacific Mail Steamship Company, 66

Panfilo de Narvaez, 86

Pantepec Petroleum Company, 122-23. *See also* William F. Buckley, Sr.

Perrin, Dr. Edward R., 51, 52, 167 nn. 43 and 46

Pershing, Brigadier General John J. ("Black Jack"), 4, 94, 168 n. 55, 172 n. 10

Peru, 89

Petatlan, Mexico, 88

CPSIA information can be obtained
at www.ICGtesting.com
Printed in the USA
LVHW040804041221
705268LV00017B/1329